DOS, DON'TS & PROFIT S

How to Buy the Right Business the Right Way

Avoid Buying the Wrong Business or the Right Business the Wrong Way

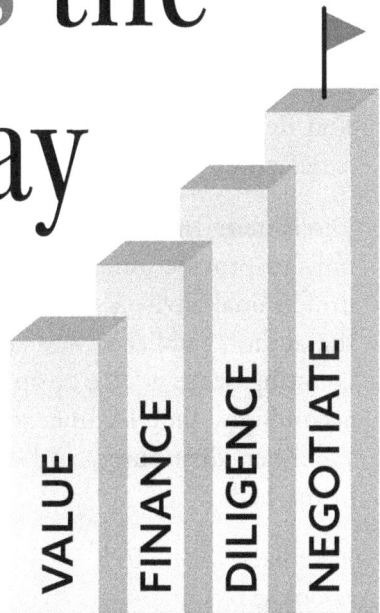

VALUE • FINANCE • DILIGENCE • NEGOTIATE

Ted J. Leverette

BUSINESS BUYER ADVOCATE®

Paperback ISBN: 978-1-7370119-2-7
eBook ISBN: 978-1-7370119-3-4
Library of Congress Control Number: 2021907972

Cover & Interior Design: Fusion Creative Works

"Partner" On-Call Network LLC can connect you to speakers for your events.

Printed in the United States of America

In Praise of the Author

Ted Leverette has hit a home run with *How to Buy the Right Business the Right Way*. Pay attention business buyers—the strategies in this book will allow you to make a great acquisition and keep you from getting a serious case of buyer fever. This is a must-read if you're even thinking of buying a business (and if you are committed to buying one, it will be a huge mistake if you don't pay attention to the tactics in this book). Above all, adhere to the overall message of buying a winner. Don't settle for anything but.

— John Martinka, author, *Buying a Business That Makes You Rich*

Recommended reading for all individuals considering buying a business - before they buy! Ted's advice is pragmatic and comprehensive.

— Tony Brown, Director | Advisor at Divest Merge Acquire, Australia

Don't forget the importance of timing. The longer you spend looking, the more it costs you, especially if you need the income.

— Richard Parker, Diomo Corporation The Business Buyer Resource Center ™

Filled with great tips for business buyers, gained from a long career of assisting buyers and sellers of hundreds of businesses. I would add one more business buying don't: Don't buy a business without reading this book.

— Steven Beal, MBA, CGA, CFA, CBV, CBI, BEAL Business Brokers & Advisors

Ted's advice on creative dealmaking is second to none. If you're going to buy a business to protect your family's future, this book is insurance you'll be glad you invested in.

— David Barnett, Author, Speaker, Educator, Business Buy/Sell Process Coach

Contents

Preface

How to Buy the Right Business the Right Way—Dos, Don'ts & Profit Strategies can help you turn your business ownership dream into a wonderful reality. But buyer beware.

A few days after buying a business, the new owner went to a fortune teller who looked into a crystal ball and said, "Owning your business will be a living nightmare for the next three years."

"And then what will happen?" the buyer hopefully asked.

"You'll get used to it"

The easiest and best way to avoid buying a loser is to get access to lots of winners . . . especially while avoiding buyer competition.

Many mistakes buyers make are errors of omission, not knowing what to do. Even people who know what to do sometimes do the wrong thing, especially if they have a bad case of buyer fever—wanting a particular business so badly they suspend their common sense.

Knowing *how* to buy is important. But, if you haven't *found* at least one (more is better) of the best businesses for sale, you may end up buying the *wrong* business. Please read my other book: *How to Prepare Yourself and Find the Right Business to Buy.*

I wouldn't be here today if I didn't almost lose all my money after I quit my fabulous job to buy the right business the wrong way. After wasting a year trying to unscramble that rotten egg and suing the seller for misrepresentation (and winning the lawsuit), I devoted myself to learning how to value and buy the right businesses the right ways. Since then, I've enjoyed twenty-eight successful small and midsize company investments.

Those experiences, and advising clients for more than thirty years, enables me to inform and guide buyers of small and midsize businesses so they can be the first choice of brokers and sellers. And avoid or beat their buyer competition. And make more-profitable done deals sooner with less aggravation at lower cost in the USA, Canada, Australia, and the U.K.

The sale and purchase of businesses seems like a good idea for sellers and buyers until things go wrong.

The first thing to understand is sellers and their advisors do not tell buyers enough of what buyers need to know to make informed decisions about buying or investing in companies.

The second thing you need to know is neither will any of your individual advisors. You need a team to safely and profitably buy or sell a small or midsize business. You must effectively participate on your team, such as gathering how-to information on your own, such as the content of this book.

What you don't know *you don't know* can hurt you.

I don't like risk. My clients don't like risk. That's why we buy mature, profitable and fairly-priced businesses that have sustainable competitive advantages.

This book can supplement what you know about buying and selling small and midsize companies. This book can be one of your best references.

Who can benefit from these books?

- *How to **Prepare** Yourself and **Find** the **Right** Business to **Buy***

- *How to **Buy** the Right Business the Right Way?*

If you are a professional advisor, business broker or other kind of intermediary involved in mergers, acquisitions or dispositions, this book can increase your effectiveness and enable your clients to achieve safer, more profitable done deals.

If you want to buy or sell a company, this book is for you. Use it in collaboration with your dealmaking advisory team.

If you are a student or early in your career wanting to know more about what occurs during real-world dealmaking, this book showcases what I and my associates have witnessed over four decades—the good, bad, and ugly.

Read my how-to books. My YouTube channel has webinars and interviews with dealmakers: https://www.youtube.com/TedLeveretteTheBusinessBuyerAdvocate

And then let me help you deploy my proven best practices.

Introduction

This book (and my other book, *How to Prepare Yourself and Find the Right Business to Buy*) is the companion to my creative financing book, *How to Get ALL the Money You Want For Your Business Without Stealing It* ™.

There's a big difference between people *wanting* to buy versus *needing* to buy a business. If what they want isn't what they need, they may not buy a business.

Buying the *right* business the *right* way is more about research and analysis than negotiating and dealmaking. The more effective your due diligence the stronger will be your advantages during negotiations and dealmaking, and the easier it will be to obtain acquisition financing.

Some of the "Don'ts" in this book are more dangerous than others.

Too many of them, which individually do not pose substantial risk, by their multitude can undermine the marketability or valuation of any business, and threaten *its* future and *your* investment.

There can be worthwhile opportunity with businesses for sale that are plagued by some of the problems among our "Don'ts."

If you are certain you can fix what management did not or could not fix, you have a negotiating edge to get better terms from the seller, and you can profit more from your investment. (Don't tell the seller your fix-it plan.)

This is not the kind of book that must be read cover-to-cover.

It's a compendium of tips, facts, and strategies, any one of which if used or ignored could pivot a pending buy/sell transaction toward success or failure. You can save time and more quickly find what you need by browsing the list of topics.

We are intentionally redundant on some topics.

It's necessary because we want you to be aware of certain dos, don'ts, and profit strategies when your business acquisition activity is occurring during phases. The most common phases are shown by this book's chapter titles.

CHAPTER 1

Some Really Big Stuff

Buyer fever.

Many mistakes business buyers make are errors of omission, not knowing what to do. Even people who know what to do sometimes do the wrong thing, especially if they have a bad case of BUYER FEVER – wanting a particular business so badly they suspend their common sense. What can cause a fatal case of buyer fever? Keep reading for details about this fatal aliment.

Beware of the sellers' marketplace.

Savvy company owners and their brokers create a seller's market by attracting multiple buyers who must compete with one another. Sometimes the dumbest buyer wins the bidding war. (This is wonderful if you're a seller.)

Don't get into bidding wars with other searchers!

The reality is too many people buy the wrong business . . . or they buy the right business but on the wrong terms.

This is what you need to know, in 8 sentences, to buy the right business the right way, sooner and with less aggravation:

1. Buying a business is all about search.

2. Because if you can't find it you can't buy it.

3.   It's about being best.

4.   And first.

5.   First on scene with sellers.

6.   And being the sellers' first choice.

7.   And top-of-mind for brokers and sellers.

8.   And, most importantly: Avoiding buyer competition!

But *searching* is not enough. This book will help you evaluate opportunities and make the deal.

Insights business buyers must detect from employees.

Beware and be aware of buyer interactions with employees. Too many people on the dealmaking playing field do not know how to adequately handle such interactions.

Business buyers, before purchasing companies, cannot perceive the company as it really is by only talking to owners and managers.

Owners and managers simply don't see it as it is.

Management is busy handling day-to-day activity and putting out fires.

Owners and managers don't have time to step back enough to see every strength that gives the company its competitive advantages *and* all the actual or pending vulnerabilities that threaten its future.

Examining employee relationships may not be as revealing as interviewing key employees.

Some buyers choose to forego interviews (especially if sellers won't permit interviews).

Some buyers believe they've adequately assessed the company. And they hope they won't be surprised after closing when employees express their opinions about their employer.

The bottom line: It comes down to balancing risk and reward.

If buyers, before completing their purchase transaction, don't interact with the seller's employees, good luck!

Bill of Rights for Buyers

Too many potential buyers of small and midsize businesses do not know what is fair and reasonable during their interaction with business sellers, business brokers, M&A intermediaries, professional service providers, sources of financing and other people and organizations they encounter during the buyers' process to locate and purchase worthwhile businesses for sale.

Uninformed potential buyers unnecessarily frustrate and complicate themselves and their relationships with the people and organizations they need the most, upon which buyers must rely to buy the right business the right way.

THE SOLUTION

Bill of Rights for Buyers of Small and Midsize Businesses

The intent of the Bill of Rights is to be perceived positively. It can be a useful educational communication for everyone on the playing field of dealmakers who seek mutual benefits.

People and companies thinking about business mergers or acquisitions can be more comfortable if they know the characteristics of the players and the boundaries of the playing field upon which dealmaking occurs.

Think "Gentlemen's Agreement," which is backed only by the integrity of the people, companies or organizations involved in a business transaction, to faithfully abide by the terms of the agreement, the basis of which is mutual respect and honorable behavior.

Despite not being legally binding, in these days of the Internet anyone feeling abused can try to make their case online.

Unrealistic expectations of inexperienced or insufficiently informed potential business buyers plus their general distrust of people who facilitate the buying of small and midsize businesses unnecessarily impede the opportunity for dealmakers and intermediaries, for buyers and sellers, their professional advisors, and for sources of financing.

A credible "Bill of Rights for Buyers of Small and Midsize Businesses" can help potential buyers know what to expect. It can provide guidelines for sellers, business brokers, M&A intermediaries, and business acquisition advisors.

Few business buyers know what should be their fair and reasonable individual rights. Many dealmakers, intermediaries, and advisors work from a Code of Ethics, but without translation and presentation in a "Bill of Rights for Business Buyers" too many buyers feel like they are flying blind.

Buyers who do not know the rules of the game of business buying flay themselves on and outside the business acquisition playing field.

Buyers, who lack specific expectations about the process to find a worthwhile business for sale, or how to buy the right business the right way, waste too much time worrying about potential abuse. Buyers' fear clouds the reputation of the dealmaking industry.

Some of us take those "rules of the game" for granted; we do not write them down or publicly show them. How can inexperienced or insufficiently informed buyers know the "rules" (i.e., best practices, reasonable expectations), and the abuses to watch out for if buyers do not know what those "rules" are?

Please see partneroncall.com for the *Bill of Rights for Buyers of Small and Midsize Businesses*.

Achieve more profitable deals.

Below are some of the topics that determine how to make a successful deal. This book delves deeply into these topics (and many more). You'll learn what's important and how to dig deeper.

- **Historical Pretax Net Profit** – Prior earnings usually are the most reliable guide as to the future expectancy. (IRS Revenue Ruling 59-60). Historical performance is important but not as important as where the business is going and how much profit it will earn.

- **Terms of Sale** – The provisions of the buy/sell contract; defining characteristics, elements and structure of the transaction.

- **Continuity of Profit** – Likelihood that the company will maintain its historical profit level without interruption into the foreseeable future, taking into account change of ownership, industry trends, etc.

- **Competition** – "Two guys are walking through the jungle when a lion appears on the path ahead of them. One of the two starts putting on a pair of running shoes. 'Why bother with running shoes?' says the first guy. 'There's no way you can outrun a lion.' 'Who said anything about outrunning a lion? says the second. 'I just want to outrun you.'" Ichak Adizes

- **Company Competitive Advantage** – Warren Buffett says the most important thing he looks for when evaluating a company is its "sustainable competitive advantage."

- **Industry** – There are no worst types of businesses, but a particular business may not be worth buying. You can make a street-smart business investment by acquiring a strong company in a temporarily troubled or declining industry.

- **Company Growth: Actual & Potential** – Some businesses are for sale because the owner does not want to make additional investments for more production capacity. Business buyers frequently overestimate the production capacity, only to discover after buying the business that it is under a low ceiling for growth.

- **Evaluate Your Marketability** – Don't confuse marketability with value. What if too few buyers want to purchase the type of business you want to buy? You could pay a "fair" price only to discover that you can't sell your business.

- **Type of Company** – Be open-minded. Just because a particular type of business appeals to you does not mean you should forego looking at others.

- **Location** – Location! Location! Location!

- **Premises and Other Tangible Assets** – How much will they contribute to or detract from the success of the company?

- **Type of Management Company Requires from its Owner** – Don't underestimate the amount of oversight that it takes to **manage a company**. Owners of small businesses (except the one you want to buy) will tell you that "passive management" is an oxymoron.

- **Intangible Enhancer to or Detractor from Value** – Goodwill, ill-will, and intellectual property, are intangible. Don't assume the business has goodwill. If a seller cannot present a buyer with a credible rationale for the value of the business' goodwill, the buyer calls it blue sky. Then the argument begins. Don't let goodwill mask ill-will.

- **Economic Outlook** – Local and national economy as it pertains to a company and its customers and its suppliers.

- **Restrictive Agreements** – Watch out for restrictive agreements, especially poorly conceived ones that invite unintended legal and tax consequences. The more severe the restrictions, the higher the (downward) adjustment to value.

I believe the *fatal flaw* for too many dealmakers is their misunderstanding of Competitive Advantage. It infects deals. It happens when the parties to the deal do not adequately put a price tag on or deduct a penalty for the elements that contribute to sustainable competitive advantages..

CIMs and CBRs.

What about Confidential Information Memorandums, Confidential Business Reviews and their variations? (Most of them are inadequate; they transfer risk to buyers.)

The best do quadruple-duty:

1. Test, upfront, the broker/seller transparency; their willingness to disclose what's most important.

2. Roadmap for due diligence.

3. Foundation of business plan, which you'll need for financing.

4. Foresee transition from seller-to-buyer.

The best CIMs enable you to focus on verification and evaluation. You won't have to waste (as much) time and money trying to pry information out brokers and sellers.

But beware. Don't let the shine blind you.

-   Is it lipstick on a pig?

Later, in this book, you'll see what you can expect (and demand) for the CIMs. Pay attention to it. You'll need details about the company to prepare your business plan, application for financing and more. If the seller does not adequately inform you, you'll have to derive all the information.

Cyber risk and security.

Too many people buying and selling small and midsize businesses are not considering cyber risks . . . and they're not doing it early enough . . . if at all.

"Cybersecurity risk on an M&A deal can end up costing you more than the purchase price you paid for the business. Not only have you paid for a business that doesn't have value, now you're in the negative territory. And that can happen when you're not doing your due diligence from this perspective when you're going to buy a business."

It gets much worse than the excerpt above, as explained during my interview with M&A attorney, **Justin Daniels**, a cybersecurity expert. He also shares tips for business buyers to help them make better deals. What he says about making sellers accountable is eye-opening. It's on my YouTube channel. https://www.youtube.com/TedLeveretteTheBusinessBuyerAdvocate

Are appraisers, advisors and business brokers negligent if they don't inform buyers and sellers of cybersecurity risk?

Keep in mind that the smaller the company and its vendors, the higher the risk.

My advice to people trying to sell or buy a small or midsize business: Detect cyber risks; otherwise you can expect blowback from your done deal.

Be authentic and reasonable transparent.

Here's a little-known trick for people searching to buy the right business the right way. Don't try to trick brokers, sellers, lenders or anyone else. If you're qualified to do the kind of deal you want, prove it. Upfront. Authenticity and transparency go a long way toward building credibility with (rightfully cynical) brokers and sellers.

And, if you don't have what it takes, get off the dealmaking playing field until you do. And trash the game plan that some charlatan sold you; you know . . . the "how-to-buy-a-wonderful-business-without-using-any-money-and-put-all-the-risk-on-the-seller."

I'm referring to transacting business with candor, provable full disclosure and free of UNFAIR self-dealing.

Brokers and sellers want to know . . . upfront . . . from searchers: What's in it for ME? Satisfaction of THEIR wants and needs!

Fulfilling the requests and expectations of brokers and sellers and their advisers and sources of referral. The savviest searchers and buyers know how to do it before being asked AND at the optimum moment.

The "I'm smarter than that guy" plan to buy a business.

This week one of my connections referred me to a YouTube presentation on how to buy a business with no money. My connection asked me how somebody who appears as inept and as inarticulate as this video presenter could possibly be taken seriously by anybody with any brains. Not to mention the unimpressed video commenters.

I think I know why unimpressive conman are able to attract viewers and then get them to pay money for their "secrets."

This presenter behaves like a nitwit. I can't imagine anybody with common sense taking him seriously. Unless . . . gullible people believe: "If this nitwit got rich doing what he says he can show me to do, and I know I'm smarter and more polished than he is, I should be able to get richer faster with less effort."

Otherwise, what's the magic that gets people to handover their hard-earned money to charlatans?

FAQs from searchers.

1. Why am I not finding *enough* of the *kinds* of businesses interest me?

2. Why am I not taken *seriously* by brokers/sellers? (Losing opportunities to buyer competition.)

3. What information *must* I get, *upfront*, to quickly/thoroughly evaluate the opportunity AND *prepare* me to apply for acquisition financing?

You can't buy it if you can't find it. Do this to prepare and find the right businesses: https://cutt.ly/bvBfpPN

It's unrealistic for searchers to expect to be taken seriously unless they do this: https://youtu.be/bK6hH0wYqbc

The savviest searchers and buyers demand this information, upfront, from brokers. And collaborate with reasonable sellers to derive it: https://www.youtube.com/watch?v=FGma2GyKlvE

The link goes to my webinar that describes what searchers are supposed to see, and also look out for. Get this right and you'll have what you want.

More reality: https://www.youtube.com/
TedLeveretteTheBusinessBuyerAdvocate

Let's Zoom if you want to talk about it,

In defense of business brokers.

Yep, by me. Surprised?

Not a week goes by that I don't hear from searchers complaining about "unrealistic" or "too-demanding" business brokers. If you had to cope what they have to go through with unqualified searchers and "buyers," you, too, might behave like some brokers.

Instead of unnecessarily burning your bridges with brokers, identify the most honest and competent brokers.

And hire the right kind of business advisor (I'm applying for the job.) and legal counsel BEFORE you begin searching for businesses to buy.

Your advisory team can tell you what's normal and customary on the dealmaking playing field.

As gatekeepers, brokers get to mostly play by their rules.

It takes realistic and savvy legal counsel plus seller/searcher/buyer flexibility to play the brokers' games.

Thinking about starting instead of buying?

Don't do it! Can you think of any industry that can benefit by the entry of another competitor? If you know how to manage employees, instead of starting, buy a mature, profitable and fairly-priced business enjoying sustainable competitive advantages.

You make money from day one and the business will continue to succeed unless you wreck it.

BTW, don't even think about starting a business if you don't know how to manage employees, plus have enough money to fund it through what will be its volatile early years.

Selecting your advisory team.

Hire people with a proven history of working for buyers and sellers of the *kind and size* of deal you intend. Ask how they have *facilitated* deals that *should* and *did* occur.

Hire deal makers, deal closers.

Avoid the wrong kind of deal killer. There are two kinds of deal killers:

- There are advisors who don't know enough about dealmaking for small and midsize companies. Not wanting to make mistakes these poseurs are more likely to poo-poo deals or, worse, bless them.

- The other kind of deal killer is adequately experienced, which means when they tell you to kill the deal, kill it.

Compatibility among team members is essential.

Searchers risk losing access to sellers or losing their money if they don't understand and know what to do about the kinds of NDAs and searcher-disclosures demanded by brokers and sellers.

Why? From a legal view, your earliest agreements with brokers and sellers materially define what you can do and expect. During negotiations and otherwise.

You can't unscramble eggs.

You can get a better result if all the members of your advisory have a future-focus; if they can help you discover and exploit opportunities instead of turning every potential risk into a life-threatening situation. Sure, it's important to detect vulnerabilities. And the best advisors can show you how to fix or live with them within an already-profitable company.

Business buyers (and sellers) can save thousands if not tens of thousands of dollars in professional fees by knowing the correct timing to handle some of the topics pertaining to reps and warranties. The savviest buyers begin certain activities while initially screening business opportunities and at the beginning of due diligence.

There's no second chance for a first impression.

Knock Knock!

Who's there?

Opportunity.

Don't be silly - opportunity doesn't knock twice!

Inadequate Zoom and telephone presence is one of the reasons why so many searchers are not taken seriously by brokers and sellers.

Sadly, only 10% of the people trying to find and buy a SMB pass my test: Zoom Presence. If you can't shine on Zoom, it's unlikely you can do it in-person.

I strongly advise searchers to deploy Zoom for their advantage. During their initial interviews of brokers and sellers.

Rehearse with me, first.

If you're not seeing enough opportunities, find out why. From my website, request my Searcher and Search Evaluation.

This entertaining 2-minute shows what the savviest searchers do: https://cutt.ly/vvV5PHs.

How bad does it get for some searchers?

Which of these pitfalls can you afford?

The terms of your LOI or offer are disclosed to people who shouldn't know about it.

The pending deal you reasonably aborted is mischaracterized, which throttles your access to more deals.

Your employment is at risk because word got out that you're trying to buy a business.

Someone who shouldn't alerts competing companies that you're hunting in their industry.

They use your confidential information to compete with you or your company.

Your finances become public knowledge.

Your applications for financing or investment are seen by people who shouldn't see them.

Disgruntled broker or seller badmouths you among people you need to favorably influence.

Owners/sellers or their representatives broadcast the fact that you're searching for opportunities.

Isn't it fair to protect the confidentiality of sensitive information about the searcher, such as employment, financial resources and perhaps even the fact that the searcher is looking for a business to buy? Anything else, which if improperly disclosed, can harm the searcher?

Tip: It's a good idea to ask your legal counsel to explain how you should conduct yourself and monitor the activity of people with whom you interact, especially people signing your NDA. What about the practicality of enforcement?

CHAPTER 2

What's Possible?

A huge wave of mature, profitable small and midsize businesses will become available for purchase over the next decade as baby boomers convert their business equity into cash. This chapter shows you how good it can be for you.

How well are you "selling" yourself to owners and sellers of companies? Or to potential lenders or investors?

The better you market yourself the more owners will want to sell their company to you and the easier it will be to get the money you need for dealmaking.

Disappointment and frustration are normal for people trying to find worthwhile businesses to buy. And it is unnecessary.

Searchers/buyers: Try thinking like owners/sellers.

How impressed would you be if a potential "buyer" behaving like you showed interest in your company for sale?

SAD, BUT TRUE, FOR HOPEFUL PEOPLE SEARCHING FOR INVESTORS OR COMPANIES . . .

More than half of the searchers asking for my *Searcher and Search Evaluation* learn that their search methods and tools are defective.

Most of them misallocated their dealmaking funds and/or they must adjust their investment objective to more realistically fit marketplace realities.

Most of them unnecessarily risk competing with other buyers.

Discovering this early is better than getting blowback from brokers, sellers, investors, and sources of financing.

Get my *Searcher and Search Evaluation*™ before you (further) expose yourself on the playing field.

Already on the playing field? Want better results?

Most business buyers searching for sellers or investors misstep during their approach to brokers, sellers, and investors.

Let me evaluate your plan to market yourself and search for deals.

"The WINNING Searcher Marketing Plan to Find Business Acquisitions"

- What You Say First to Brokers, Owners and Sellers

- Pitch Deck (written presentation for face-to-face or online meetings)

- Acquisition Criteria

- Methodology/Process (especially timing, targeting and follow-up scripts)

- Search (prospecting, letter, email, etc.)

- Resume

- Link(s) to your online presence (even if it does not pertain to your search).

- Letter of Interest

- NDA and Letter of Intent (Heads of Terms for U.K.)

- Response Rate and Worthiness of Responses

Tip: What you voice first to brokers, owners and sellers either repels them or motivates them to talk to you.

Deliverables / Benefits

Diagnosis and evaluation.

Identification and explanation of searchers' (actual and pending) activities that do not serve their self-interest.

Motivation and direction to improve what people do during search. Why me?

I evaluate searchers and search methodologies in the context of hundreds of done deals. My colleagues have shared information about thousands of searchers and dealmakers.

I have no businesses to sell or recommend.

No conflict of interest. My loyalty is solely to buyers looking for opportunities leading to done deals.

Get started right.

One of the most crucial things in searching for a company to buy is to get started right. You only have one chance to make a favorable first impression. If you don't have all the components in place before you meet the owner of a good business, you could blow your chance to buy it.

It comes down to this: I don't know your dreams, but most people say they need more money or more control over their worklife. Some people need big money, to put their kids through college or to fund their retirement. Others want to be rich(er). Some people simply want to have more spending money and are willing to work hard to get it.

What's it worth to you to know how to find the right business and to know what to do when you find it?

What's it worth to you to make the amount of money you want, and to control your worklife?

What's it worth to you to finally become what you've dreamed?

What's it worth to you to be able to do it now, by taking steps that others have perfected over the years?

This book can be one of the tools that help you achieve the success you seek.

But don't let do-it-yourself thinking slow you down or increase your risk. Why risk everything by trying to cut a few corners or by isolating yourself from the street-smart experience of a business acquisition advisory team whose sole purpose is to protect you and to maximize your profit?

Imagine you are taking up skydiving. You attend a pre-jump lecture, and then learn how to pack your parachute.

Would you say this to the instructor? "Thanks for the lecture on how to pack my chute, jump and then land. See ya later!" And then board the airplane by yourself? Flash to reality. Wouldn't you expect your instructor to accompany you on board the airplane, to build your confidence while the plane is moving into position, to encourage you to jump, and possibly to make the first jump a tandem one, where you and the expert do it together, so you land safely, with both feet firmly on the ground?

Buying a business is like sky diving. It can be lots of fun or it can kill you.

This book shows how sellers and their advisors plan to sell you a business and the strategies they employ to influence you. While safely reading this book, you learn about mistakes most people make, so you don't make them in the real world with wasted time and money.

With the knowledge from one or more members of your team, as you get started or as you dig deeper into the deal before you, you're increasing your odds that you can make a profitable investment and get more control over your worklife.

You could be the best carpenter in the world, but what can you build without a toolbox? This book is one of your moneymaking tools. Your business acquisition advisory team helps you implement what you read in this book, and beyond.

This book develops the big strategies; it warns you and encourages you. And it explains how to implement some of what you need to do. But it's like reading and then trying to cook a recipe. The food probably won't taste like you thought it would until several tries, if ever, even if you use the right amount of all the ingredients and use the right amount of heat for the right amount of time. It's all in the technique, the methodologies. You can practice with your time and money, or your advisory team can help you do what works.

A much more comprehensive presentation of this chapter appears in my other book: *How to Prepare Yourself and Find the Right Business to Buy*.

CHAPTER 3

One Word Distinguishes Successful Business Buyers

According to the top intermediaries and advisors, 93% of people wanting to buy or merge small or midsize companies fail to do so. Most of them don't even make it to third base.

Just one word differentiates the winners from the losers who **do** and who **don't** buy small and midsize companies.

Most people don't know what it is.

How do I know? I surveyed 10,000 people. Nearly all of them are buy/sell dealmakers or their representatives or advisors. And some of them are failing wannabes. So far, they have suggested and explained more than 60 important attributes, which can result in done deals.

One word is the common denominator: Guts!

Why do we know this? Our 500-year collective experience working for acquirers as their *Business Buyer Advocate*.

We also surveyed 10,000 people on the buy/sell playing field: Acquirers, attorneys, accountants, appraisers, brokers, and sources of financing. We also communicated with failing wannabes.

The MOST important attribute may not be what you think it is.

And guess what? Most of the people, proposing the one word, were wrong. Not my opinion; theirs, after I explained the rationale for the MOST important characteristic.

What some of us believe to be the *most* indispensable characteristic may upset the usual thinking of some people, including professional advisors.

First, winners achieve done deals. And that happens because they stay the course. This happens because they bring to the deal-making playing field as many or more than 60 attributes, just one of which empowers everything else. If that one attribute, guts, is missing or weak, people probably won't buy a business.

You can read about all the attributes that distinguish and empower the most successful buyers of businesses in my book: *How to Prepare Yourself and Find the Right Business to Buy—Dos, Don'ts & Profit Strategies*. It's available from my website.

This information can educate people who want to achieve a done deal; it can also help their advisors. Advisors? Sure. Winning professional reputations are made when advisors enable clients to succeed. Advisors make more money from clients that progress all the way to a done deal. Some of you can use my books for your self-assessment.

Why is this important? I don't know anyone who wants to fail. Do you? And too many people fail because they don't have what it takes for success.

CHAPTER 4

Due Diligence

Better SAD now than sad later!

Seek—

Substantiation

Accountability

Disclosure

Thorough pre-acquisition due diligence of the company's value and risk increases the probability that you will buy the right business the right way. With each potential acquisition, begin by establishing your primary point of contact, which is someone who knows enough about the business to accompany you throughout your evaluation of the company. This person should help you gather relevant documents and help you schedule interviews of people within and outside the company.

This chapter shows how to do it, so you can avoid pitfalls along the way.

The most important two senses that you can employ throughout due diligence are an eye for detail and a nose for deceit. Most of the problems that can come back to haunt you were in plain sight while you were doing your due diligence.

— Stephen J. Kerr

Definition and use of "due diligence."

Due diligence is the investigation of a business to confirm that it is what someone says it is and that it is worth what the buyer is willing to pay.

Due diligence "officially" begins when you decide upon the content of your nonbinding letter of intent (to purchase a business) or the provisions of a contractual offer to purchase, whichever comes first. The scope of your letter of intent or purchase offer usually determines the process for due diligence. Your investigation provides you with information, so you (and your advisors) can make informed decisions. These decisions relate to

- Go & no-go (continue the process or abandon the transaction).

- Deal structure (including acquisition and post-purchase financing).

- Business valuation.

Skimping on due diligence will cost you.

Simple in definition but essential to your wellbeing. Due diligence simply means the investigation of a business "to confirm that the company is what the seller says it is; that it is worth the price the buyer is paying; free from contingent or unknown liabilities; and capable of continuing as represented." Source: Anthony A. King, a lawyer with the firm of Minor & Brown, P.C. in Denver, CO.

"Hunting the big deal killers first."

There are lots of self-defeating behaviors by searchers and owners that tank deals that should occur. But there is something worse: deals that should not have occurred. Finding out, after closing/completion, that it is a dumb deal costs sellers and buyers.

- Buyers may sue sellers, refuse to pay them, etc.

- Buyers can lose more money than the price they paid for the company. Lots more.

BTW, "hunting the big deal killers first" comes from an article from the website of CPA, **Kevin Bassett**.

Beware of the pandemic and stimulus money.

Beware of the consequences from the flood of stimulus money dispersed to consumers and companies. It caused a spending splurge on various goods and services. So-called "essential businesses" continued to perform well; some better than ever. But other, struggling, sectors held on thanks to temporary support by governments. Lots of M&A dumb deals were made, even for the smallest privately held businesses. Ill-informed and ill-advised buyers recklessly bid against each other, driving up the prices of some of the businesses for sale. At the time thus book is being written, it remains to be seen whether the higher pricing multiples can be sustained. Will the bubble burst?

The pandemic is no excuse for searchers not to interview key employees of businesses for sale. One of the most important tactical benefits for sellers AND buyers is the ability for searchers to learn more about the employees, especially the key employees. Interviewing some of them is important, but only under tightly controlled conditions; searchers who don't know when and how to do it can undermine the value of the business and stifle any kind of buy/sell agreement. This is "killing the goose that lays the golden eggs."

Sellers/vendors can tempt searchers by confidentially showing searchers the employee performance evaluation reports, concealing the name of the employees. And maybe only the key employees.

(What? There are no written evaluation reports? Wonder what else is wrong with the business.)

Proceed in haste; regret at leisure.

Evaluate the strength of the supply chain.

Beware and be aware of the supply chain.

Are there potential or actual adverse effects on the supply chain caused by shortages or shipping delays, perhaps due to raw materials, politics or economics?

What about the affect on pricing when the supply and demand ratio changes?

What about contractual liabilities, such as shipment and delivery requirements?

The automotive sector, for example, during the 2020-2021 Covid pandemic could not get one kind of semiconductor. Production of certain vehicles was stopped, leaving hanging dealers and customers.

Traps and Risks of NDAs and PGs.

How much are you aware of these two traps and risks for buyers *and* sellers of businesses? The first begins with the Non-Disclosure Agreement (NDA) and the second arises later regarding the Personal Guarantee (PG).

Spoiler alert:

- Naive searchers/buyers sign NDAs and PGs foisted on them.

- Unreasonable demands by sellers repel the savviest and perhaps the best-qualified buyers.

They do it because they don't know what they don't know. They simply (and mistakenly) believe they're supposed to do it.

Both legal documents are negotiable if you know how to do it.

Below are my notes from talking to M&A attorney, **Scott Weavil**, weavillaw.com, about NDAs. What he says can help business buyers avoid pitfalls, which I've too-often seen. Especially where *mutuality* is absent from NDAs foisted on searchers.

- Owners/sellers and their representatives broadcast the fact that you're searching for opportunities.

- The terms of your LOI or offer is disclosed to people who shouldn't know about it.

- The pending deal you reasonably aborted is mischaracterized, which throttles your access to more deals.

- Your employment is at risk because word got out that you're trying to buy a business.

- Someone who shouldn't alerts competing companies that you're hunting in their industry.

- They use your confidential information to compete with you or your company.

- Your finances become public knowledge.

- Your applications for financing or investment are seen by people who shouldn't see them.

- Disgruntled broker or seller badmouths you among people you need to favorably influence.

It's a good idea to ask your legal counsel to explain how you should conduct yourself and monitor the activity of people with whom you interact, especially people signing your NDA. What about the practicality of enforcement?

Raise your guard if you see this in CIMs and CBRs.

Sometimes it's a living nightmare for searchers trying to find worthwhile businesses for sale. That's thanks to inadequate Confidential Information Memorandums, Confidential Business Reviews and their variations.

EXAMPLES

"Management has elected to omit substantially all the disclosures and the statement of cash flow's required by accounting principles gener-ally accepted in the United States of America. If the omitted disclosures and the statement of cash flows were included in the financial state-ments, they might influence the users conclusions about the company's

financial position, results of operations, and cash flow's. Accordingly, the financial statements are not designed for those who are not informed about such matters."

"Explain your key assumptions used to arrive at your offering price."

"What are your material assumptions, which explain your offer or valuation?"

- Broker/seller wants to know and discuss this with you before you can move forward. It is incredibly stupid for searchers, upfront, to reveal their rationale.

"[Buyer], if Seller doesn't, will pay broker full commission provided in the Listing Agreement."

- It's not a good idea to let sellers/brokers transfer their risk and/or liability to the purchaser. Watch out for limited liability in NDAs and CIMs.

We will have about 15 buyers interested in being the buyer for this business."

- How about that for chutzpah!

Mostly, searchers are underwhelmed with the first presentation package, which supposedly represents the businesses for sale. And not just their poor display, typos and nonsense.

Too often, CIMs and their ilk are so deficient or misleading that searchers want to walk away.

And sometimes that's the best decision. And sometimes it's not.

Keep in mind:

It will take a long time to do a deal unless you know, upfront, how to handle presentations, which upon first impression repel you.

The best CIMs and CBRs fully disclose.

You saw some of this earlier in this book. It's worth repeating. Your risk increases if you don't get what you need, upfront, from brokers and sellers.

Here's the minimum you need to see to be adequately informed:

INTRODUCTION
- About the Business Broker
- Instructing Buyers
- Executive Summary
- Key Acquisition Highlights

GENERAL INFORMATION
- Business Overview
- Business History
- Business Timeline
- Product/Service Range
- Customer Profile
- Supplier Profile
- Systems & Processes
- Strategic Direction
- Business Ownership
- Internal Structure
- Competitive Strategic Advantages

LOCATION
- Strategic Position
- Maps & Distances
- Local Demographics
- Business Premises
- Lease Agreement
- Photo Gallery

ACQUISITION
- Asset Schedule

- Intellectual Property
- Licenses & Permits

FINANCIAL INFORMATION
- Financial Summary
- Ownership Shares Trading History
- Monthly Trailing Cash Flow Report (36-months)
- Balance Sheet
- Profit & Loss Statement (3-years)
- Adjustments Explained
- Add-back Adjustments
- Financial Analysis and Trends

ADDITIONAL INFORMATION
- Competitive Analysis
- Industry Report

SWOT ANALYSIS
- SWOT Analysis Explained
- SWOT ANALYSIS
- Business Strengths
- Business Weaknesses
- Business Opportunities
- Business Threats

CONCLUSION
- Concluding Message
- Next Steps
- Get In Touch

DISCLAIMERS & NOTICES

ACKNOWLEDGEMENT BY SELLER

There are various levels of disclosure for CIMs and CBRs.

One of the brokers I most respect, an Australian, **Tony Brown**, divestmergeacquire.com, commented on LinkedIn about Investment Memorandums: *"The IM should be the virtual 'walk though' of the business, providing answers to the most expected 80% of items a target investor would want to know, to decide whether it's worth exploring further or not. If you were buying a house, you'd be able to readily see 80% of what you need to know, with a building and pest inspection and a lawyer to cover the other items. When buying a business, a walk through tells you very little - e.g. whether the business has one site or many, one customer or many, one product or many, profitable or not, how many employees. The IM should provide this virtual 'walk through'. Without it, both buyer and sellers would waste a lot of time asking and responding to basic questions every target investor would want to know."*

Beware of CIMs and CBRs.

Yes, it's rare for searchers to see, upfront, well-written, finely-crafted CIMs/CBRs that adequately disclose information about businesses for sale.

My YouTube channel shows how I dissect the worst and the best CIMs, so you can judge the scope and transparency of what brokers/sellers present to influence you. https://www.youtube.com/TedLeveretteTheBusinessBuyerAdvocate

Here's what people are saying about the webinars. You'll glean tips from their comments.

Attorney: The CIM was a great example. If only every deal had one like it that prompted many of the right questions. Very helpful. In fact, a lot of brokers would be happy for buyers to have less info than in that CIM at the conclusion of diligence.

Searcher: I see why brokers and sellers won't like some of what you say. And that's why everyone thinking about buying a business needs to hear you. Let's hope your effort to educate causes sellers to be more

transparent and truthful. And brokers to prepare better-described and better-written offerings.

Searcher: As you went through the CIM, you explained the good points, the good illustrations and pictures and also pointed out details that either needed improvement or were lacking pertinent information. The presentation was well-done and a fair assessment. And, a good guideline for brokers to consider. It was a nice walk through.

Searcher: I found this to be VERY valuable. I loved that you shared the CIM and that you untangled the pieces and gave comments on exactly what to look for. I only have requested a couple from brokers, and nothing I have received has been this extensive.

Business Advisor: Many thanks. It's obvious that you know your subject inside out and you covered a lot of valuable advice for a potential purchaser of the business. You also gave me some additional thoughts on how my services can be helpful for purchasers of a business. It was an excellent way to spend an hour and very valuable.

Searcher: The CIM format you showed was above and beyond anything I've seen. I have seen long templates before though and they are almost always computer generated for the most part. I've caught several mathematical errors because of this and let the brokers know to change them. I'm glad you mentioned the add-back of salary because I just had another broker do this. That was one of the questions I wanted to ask – calibrating down to reality the broker and owner. That is a necessity, and it is difficult to know when that must occur. No one wants to waste time.

Searcher: Definitely worthwhile, as usual. Seeing an example of a professionally built and presented CIM sure does shine a light on what a person could expect, versus what you typically see. If I were a seller, this is exactly how I would want to position my business for sale. I can imagine the value this would provide the buyer as well as their entire team assisting in the purchase. Particularly the case of a DIY buyer with an inexperienced banker, accountant and lawyer, this adds so much value. As a buyer the information you receive contained in that pack-

age adds an incredible amount of validity to the seller's proposition and answers many of the questions you'd want to ask. Certainly you will want to validate the claims but for a the right business, their effort is likely to speed up the entire process or getting to offer, and closing a deal. Interesting guidance on the disclaimer that the broker has no liability. The repercussions to that agreement, particularly if the seller should provide guidance with respect to any adverse change in business yet without any true responsibility to disclose such info, was interesting; a detail that many people could surely miss while contained in such a professional and polished document. This detail alone is proof that going it alone, can prove costly.

Searcher: I thoroughly enjoyed the presentation and the identification of the issues in the CIM. I loved the way that you commented on each of the issues within the page and your comments were succinct. I appreciated that the CIM you chose was one of the better ones. I have seen a good number that are really pitiful.

Searcher: The presentation was well done. Your straight forwardness saves me a lot of time. This presentation is probably well-suited for individuals who have more than a cursory knowledge of the process; it would have been over the head of a newbie. Your C.E.L.B.S. acronym is valuable insight.

Attorney: Having a checklist approach on due diligence (the facts behind the puffery) is great. Very informative. Very comprehensive (each deal presents its own nightmares). Having your broker do what Ted suggests is a real advantage. For lawyers, bottom line is: buyers should have no binding obligation before signing purchase agreement, except an NDA (limited by term); on the other hand, I don't expect sellers to be bound by reps and warranties until LOI—even then bound only by an exclusivity clause and mutual NDA, but not reps. So, I am not bothered by disclaimers, unless they waste the buyer's time. In fact, they provide targets: CIM says X, so tell me about X.1, X.2. Just off the top of my head, it seems that whether a CIM is helpful or unhelpful depends on the diligence of the intermediary that produces it, and that intermediary can be limited in what they can do based on the level of sophistication of the selling company in terms of having and being able to communicate the information most relevant to buyers. By the time we lawyers see CIMs, the buyer has decided to invest in a lawyer, and at that stage CIMs do help inform us and allow us to focus on prioritizing diligence questions. But I sense that your webinar is dealing with the preceding phase, when the buyer is evaluating CIMs as part of the process of screening a number of target candidates. I suppose lawyers could be useful at that stage, but unless we regularly represent serial buyers, we often aren't usually brought in at that stage.

Here's where some of the best business brokers go to see and create the best-of-the best formats: **BBMS MEDIA** (Marketing for Business Brokers) http://bbms.media/business-profiles.php.

Pay attention to it because you'll need details about the company to prepare your business plan, application for financing and more. If the seller does not adequately inform you, you'll have to derive all the information.

The best do quadruple-duty:

- Test, upfront, the broker/seller transparency; their willingness to disclose what's most important.

- Roadmap for due diligence.

- Foundation of business plan, which you'll need for financing.

- Foresee transition from seller-to-buyer.

But beware. Don't let the shine blind you.

- Is it lipstick on a pig?

What about Quality of Earnings?

One of the most valuable things I do with my clients is narrow their focus on where they need legal and accounting expertise. Unless you like writing blank checks for advice, it's especially important to do your own evaluation about Quality of Earnings before you assign work to advisors. https://corporatefinanceinstitute.com/resources/knowledge/deals/quality-of-earnings-report/

Begin with realistic expectations and goals.

Unrealistic or uninformed expectations can be unnecessarily troublesome, for you and everyone else. It's said that up to 95% of wannabe buyers don't buy a business. The sad truth is some of these buyers waste a considerable amount of money during their failed attempts to find and purchase a company. Some of them deplete too much of their life savings, which means they cannot afford to acquire a company. Wasting money on deals that fall through adversely affects the buyers' financial security. You can avoid these unfortunate outcomes if, before you begin hunting for sellers, you thoroughly research the industries in which your target companies do business. See publicly available industry ratios, which will assist you in benchmarking a target company's financial performance against industry norms.

According to the Institute of Business Appraisers, the best proof of the value of a business is the sale price. Numerous (and credible) sources of buy/sell stats are available; besides reporting selling prices the best databases reveal the key terms of the buy/sell transaction. One of these information providers compiles and reports information on up to 88 data points highlighting the financial and transactional details of the sales of privately and closely held companies. Buyers lacking such insight are hobbled by their unrealistic expectations.

Don't start with the touchy issues.

Begin your due diligence with the easy issues, especially the ones that are likely to present the business in its best light. This lulls the seller into thinking that you're on the hook; he may not invite other buyers to see what he has to offer. Move quickly through the good news topics and then work on the tough, controversial issues.

20 caution signals buyers must detect.

Think seriously about walking away, especially if too many of these raise their ugly head.

Incompetent or obnoxious broker, seller, or their advisory team.

The company does not match your acquisition criteria.

You're not fully qualified to manage and grow the company.

Broker or seller demands a nonbinding letter of intent that is too specific or too inclusive.

Broker or seller expects the buyer to contract prematurely (even with contingencies).

No compelling reason to sell.

General unwillingness to candidly discuss the business' condition and reason for sale.

The business is losing money.

The business is growing faster than it can finance its growth; it's dependent upon banks.

Unrealistic price.

Down payment requirement is beyond the buyer's capability.

Seller financing is not available for at least 10% of the purchase price.

Seller wants the seller financing to be repaid too quickly.

Seller wants the buyer to pledge too much personal collateral or for too long.

Unrealistic other terms of sale, such as non-compete, consulting or employment agreements.

The company is plagued with customer service problems.

Incomplete or inadequate records.

Premises lease expires before the buyer can recoup his investment in the business.

The seller can't explain the advantages his business has over its competitors.

Seller won't agree to a reasonable plan for transitioning ownership post-closing/completion.

Use checklists and data-gathering/analysis forms.

Use checklists so you don't forget anything important. The checklists can keep you on track; they remind you of actions you can take and questions you can ask.

Don't be blind to industry standards.

No business is an island. Don't buy a company unless you understand its industry. What occurs among similar businesses can affect your business. Therefore, invest a considerable amount of quality time evaluating the industry and the competitors most likely to affect the company you might buy. Compare the company with its industry standards, as an aid in diagnosing its health and in forecasting its future.

Here are some databases that may be useful to you and your advisors. (Google the titles to learn about them.)

- Business Reference Guide – The Essential Guide to Pricing a Business

- IBA Market Data – Business Sales

- BIZCOMPS˚

- DoneDeals˚ / Mid-Market Comps

- DealStats (formerly Pratt's Stats)

- RMA Annual Statement Studies˚ Valuation Edition

- IRS Corporate Ratios

Caveat: The reported selling prices do not necessarily reflect valuation. They're a function of who's buying, what they're buying, and the terms of sale materially affect selling prices. Prices also fluctuate in response to local and national economic conditions and the availability and terms of financing.

Know your business and industry
better than anyone else in the world.

— *Mark Cuban*

Don't minimize industry immaturity.

All businesses and industries have a life cycle. The pecking order of businesses in some industries is so well established it is nearly impossible to grow a company's revenue by adding customers. The owners of these businesses, therefore, increase profit with a combination of price increases, new products and services, cost reduction, acquisition of competitors and merging with synergistic companies.

Don't be blind to neighboring businesses.

Early in your investigation of any business, find out how other nearby businesses are doing. Don't just ask people; observe traffic and shopping habits. You might learn that numerous types of businesses in the neighborhood are faltering because of changes in the local society or economy.

Don't be limited to financial analysis.

The truth about a business relates to the nonfinancial factors that influence value, such as the business' relationship with its employees, customers, suppliers, landlord and sources of financing.

Scrutinize C.E.L.B.S. ™

Did you interview the *C.E.L.B.S.* before and immediately after purchasing?

Due diligence does not simply mean looking at financial statements. Perhaps more important are the non-financial factors. I coined an acronym, "*C.E.L.B.S.*," to refer to them. This relates to the quality of the business' relationships with its customers, employees, landlord, bank, and suppliers. Financial statements merely tell you where the business has been. Historical financial records can erroneously imply where the business is headed. You will discover the truth about a business, and its future, if you evaluate the non-financial factors.

Don't forget to search online for info about the seller, the company and its key employees, customers, suppliers, etcetera.

Don't waste time on a dumb deal.

Contender or pretender? Look for another business to buy if it does not match your acquisition criteria. You may not know this until you begin to verify the seller's representations. It pays to expedite the seller's production of documents for your review. A *Business Buyer Advocate* can show you how to quickly get relevant facts so you can screen out businesses not worth buying. Time is money.

But what about when the seller's representations are inconsistent with reality, when the seller is not trying to fraudulently induce you into making an offer? Eyes wide open is a good rule. What you are told should be consistent with what you see. If not, why not?

Our investments continue to be few and simple in concept:

The truly big investment idea can usually be explained in a short paragraph. We like a business with enduring competitive advantages that is run by able and owner-oriented people. When these attributes exist, and when we can make purchases at sensible prices, it is hard to go wrong.

— *Warren Buffett*

Don't fall for the fallacy of passive ownership.

Don't underestimate the amount of oversight that it takes to manage a passive investment. "This business nearly runs itself." "You can manage this business from your hammock because its manager is so good." About the time that you discover problems is the time when you must fire the manager and hope to get the business back on course. Owners of small businesses (except the one you want to buy) will tell you that "passive management" is an oxymoron.

The "worth" myth can fool you.

What's it worth to you? Certain people ask this when they want to sell a business to you. It's usually so you will take your eye off the "value" ball. There are many psychic benefits of business ownership. But, if you are going to pay money for the business, the business should have a capability to provide you with a good living and a reasonable return on your investment. Business is a financial function. Your family will not be pleased to hear from you someday that the business you bought made you happy but adversely affected your net worth.

Understand the power of the principal.

Part of the payment you make to retire debt is applied to principal (the rest is interest). Each principal payment is like making a deposit into your savings account; it builds your net worth if the business makes the payment from its profit instead of you withdrawing personal savings to make the payment.

Don't trust the claim of "no selling required."

"Our product is so good that it sells itself." "Our location is so good that it attracts customers for us." Uh huh. A seller who promises or infers easy revenue with no overt marketing and salesmanship is scamming you. Good products and a convenient location are not enough to sustain a business. Your competitors will make offers to your customers that are more appealing than what you offer. Marketing and salesmanship are necessary to compete.

Cash flow doesn't trump profit.

Business is about cash flow! Negative cash flow can kill a profitable company. Make detailed cash flow projections. Update them before, during and after you buy the business and before and after you make material changes to it. Keep notes of your underlying assumptions. There's an old saw: If you mind your pennies, the dollars will take care of themselves. On the other hand, if you focus excessively on the pennies, you might miss out on the big bucks.

Every rough diamond is not a potential gem.

Some rough diamonds are merely rough diamonds. The Don'ts in this book can help you see the imperfections. And your acquisition team can help you chip away at them to create a nice investment. Or move on.

Distressed businesses needn't turn you away.

What ails a business may give you a fabulous opportunity. This is particularly relevant if you already own a business that is like a troubled one for sale. Could you merge it into your business or diversify it?

Avoid being scammed.

If it's too good to be true it probably isn't. Do not think law enforcement or the courts will enable you to recoup your loss. Scammers are pros. They have good legal advice; they know how to steal from you without penalty. Watch the evening news if you doubt this.

Don't skip the background check; do it early.

It is easy. You can do it yourself in a few hours with minimal cost. Don't underestimate the importance of determining integrity of the seller, key employees, and other important stakeholders. You could regret it if you fail to accurately judge it in advance.

Here are some ways to evaluate a company or person: Check credit history. Do a litigation search by checking with the courts. Examine the complaints at the Better Business Bureau, the Department of Consumer Affairs and the Attorney General's office. If you uncover scary information, and you still want to buy the business, your lawyer and others can do a more thorough investigation; they can suggest additional due diligence and draft provisions in your purchase contract to protect you.

Be a welcome guest in the seller's company.

You undoubtedly will find fault with the company, its employees and maybe its customers and suppliers. But you do not have to voice it in their presence. Confer with your acquisition team about when and how to communicate bad news, especially criticism.

Don't hire jerks or deal killers.

Some advisors operate on the principle that they can be blamed or sued if you make a bad investment while they are on your dime. So, they unnecessarily toss banana peels under most, if not all, potential deals. You cannot blame them for your buying mistake if you do not buy a business. It is essential that you ask around to identify the deal facilitators. Did I mention that the deal killers don't mind charging you a lot of money? Or that the jerks repel legitimate, worthwhile sellers, business brokers and the advisors working for sellers?

You, when beginning, don't have to know everything.

Yes, the more you know about the potential acquisition and deal-making the lower your risk and the higher your profit. Therefore, focus on finding answers as you go along; effective research can be the key to a winning deal.

Don't undervalue the #2 employee.

Does the company employ a competent second-in-command employee?

It can be dangerous to purchase an owner-operator kind of company. It can be difficult to transition into a business where the seller was the owner-manager. If you have sufficient capital to purchase a business wherein the former owner did not do too much of the non-managerial work, your chances for success rise. At the minimum strive for companies that have a second-in-command employee who is well-experienced and competent. Otherwise, you could be so busy working in the business that you do not have enough time to improve the business.

Don't overestimate production capacity.

Production capacity refers to how much work you can expect employees to perform reasonably and competently. It also relates to how much volume of business can be generated by the machinery, equipment, vehicles, and facilities. The availability of working capital affects production capacity. Some businesses are for sale because the owner does not want to make an additional investment for more production capacity. Business buyers frequently overestimate the production capacity, only to discover after buying the business that it is under a low ceiling for growth. If the buyer cannot raise the funds to expand capacity and increase marketing, competitors will probably move in on the opportunity.

Buy a company that has been profitable at least 3 years.

Your investment is likely to be safer and more profitable if you buy a business that has been profitable for at least the previous three years before you buy it. There are numerous fairly priced businesses for sale that have a history of strong profit. They are available all the time and in every industry.

Buyers who have the patience to find and purchase winners tend to do better than buyers who expect the company's future to improve. Buyers have only themselves to blame when they acquire a company with a volatile or unprofitable history or future.

Don't rely on representations by the sellers' advisors.

The worst acquisition I made is because I naively believed the seller's big-name law firm and accounting firm. They knew how to lie in ways that made it nearly impossible for me to seek redress from them after I bought the business and discovered their foul play. Verify!

Step back to see the big picture.

Don't neglect scope. Most wannabe business buyers rightfully and intensely focus on what is in front of them. But few people sufficiently step back and examine scope. Simultaneously seeing details *and* scope is essential to maximize success and minimize risk. You wouldn't want to have purchased a highly profitable business in an industry that was about to be devastated, would you? It happens every day.

Don't be bullied during due diligence.

It takes time to bake a cake and it takes time to thoroughly research and to verify what the seller tells you and gives you. Don't accept a short fuse for due diligence. (Some brokers and sellers won't permit more than 10 days, which is ridiculous.) Don't let anyone fail to give you a complete answer to every reasonable question you ask.

Don't be fooled by cooked books.

Don't fail to detect the illegal and the legal ways sellers cook the books. It is easy for a business owner to temporarily change the business' usual operating policies and procedures or to adjust the financial statements. Businesses can do so without violating the law. Their intent is to misleadingly inflate the business' net cash flow and/or net profit. These actions can mortgage the future of the business. Like time bombs their detrimental effect does not show up right away.

A few tactics business sellers use to inflate market value: deplete inventory; defer asset maintenance and repair; neglect to upgrade assets, staffing or marketing below level of competition; classify owner compensation and perks as business profit; reduce labor cost with fewer or cheaper employees; discount the price (or offer special terms) of a product to a level that cannot be profitably sustained.

Don't assume the company owns the assets you see.

Verify that the firm has unencumbered title to its assets. Tangibles, such as vehicles, furnishings and equipment, and intangibles such as trademarks, patents, and copyrights. Related, carefully assess the terms of all leases.

Don't unknowingly be handcuffed.

Has the business granted or promised any franchise, license, or distributorship agreement? Relationships such as these can provide good leverage for the company that grants them. However, make sure that this type of agreement complies with the law and does not handcuff the business' ability to change its operating practices or increase revenue.

Don't assume info won't be "stolen" by competitors.

Don't be lulled into complacency by the "protection" the company says it has for its proprietary trade secrets, patents, trademarks, copyrights, and license agreements. Confer with a good intellectual property attorney before you invest in a business that relies heavily on its proprietary technology.

Don't assume competitors can't legally usurp "proprietary" technology.

According to *Bloomberg News*, Checkpoint Systems Inc., which makes anti-embezzlement security tags, said a U.S. court invalidated a patent it was seeking to enforce against All-Tag Security SA and Tyco International Ltd.'s Sensormatic Electronics. Checkpoint, the biggest maker of radio frequency tags used to prevent shop-lifting sued the two companies, claiming patent infringement. (Checkpoint may appeal.)

Do you have the expertise and financial means to get into a court battle to protect your rights? A court fight is risky and expensive; it may put you out of business.

Consider TiVo woes. TiVo invented a revolutionary digital recording device to record TV shows and zap commercials. Because of knockoffs, which TiVo's competitors sell, TiVo won't be able to retain its dominant share of the market.

Look for infringement of intellectual property.

The company you want to buy shouldn't be illegally infringing on anyone else's intellectual property. And nobody should be infringing on its proprietary property.

Imagine you bought a company, and then you were contacted by an attorney accusing your company of illegally infringing on her client's trade secrets, patents, copyrights, or trademarks. Imagine what you would have to do to rectify the situation, and the cost thereof. Imagine your conversation about this with the former owner who did not disclose to you the company's infringement.

One quick and easy way to begin finding infringements on a company's intellectual property is to Google phrases that describe the trade secrets, patents, copyrights, and trademarks. For example, *BIZFIZBO* ˚ (business for sale by-owner), is one of my registered trademarks. Searching online for "BIZFIZBO" should show only references pertaining to me, my business enterprises, and the people legally authorized by me to use that tradename.

Alexandra Clough, in the *Palm Beach Post*, "Nike to CrossFit CityPlace: That one-armed handstand logo is ours," writes: Can a one-arm handstand ever be mistaken for a basketball slam-dunk? Nike says yes, and the global sneaker maker is suing CrossFit CityPlace in West Palm Beach over CrossFit's one-arm handstand logo. The shoe, apparel and merchandising conglomerate says the upside [down] image of a man balanced on a kettle bell is too similar to its signature "jump-man," logo, a depiction of basketball great Michael Jordan. Of course, that iconic Nike mark is of a man leaping, hand gripped on a basketball, and not balancing upside down on one arm. But no matter. Nike opposes CrossFit CityPlace's effort to trademark its logo because it believes the logo is too similar to "jump-man." Nike says the CityPlace CrossFit logo will create confusion with the public, causing the sneaker maker "grave and irreparable damage. "They're trying to bully the little guy because they've got more money," says the accused owner of CrossFit CityPlace.

Let's hope that none of us must cope with something like this!

Asking naive questions invites misdirection.

When you interview, with the seller's advance written permission, the key customers, employees, sources of financing, landlord and suppliers, do not merely ask if they are happy with their relationship with the seller's company. Ask whether they intend to retain their relationship on the present terms. And if not, why not? Maybe ask: Why do you choose to do business with this company?

The business does not have to be number one.

In business, as in the entertainment industry, the second fiddle does quite well. Don't shy away from a good business with a steady cash flow simply because it is not at the top of the heap of competitors. A business does not have to be a shining star for it to be a good acquisition for you and for it to provide the emotional and financial security you desire.

Don't let your perception blind you.

How we perceive things is affected by our training, experience, and values. Most corporate mergers and acquisitions are not what their principals hoped they would be for one reason: cultural incompatibility. When you are buying a company, you are buying into the ways of doing business within the company and within its industry. You are also buying into the lifestyle, attitudes, and customs of the societal community in which the company is located. If you're a Yankee relocating to the south or if you're an urbanite moving to the country, proceed with caution. If you're new to a community, it's best to keep your advisors from back home in the background; employ locals for the unique benefits they provide. It's not fun to be a stranger in a strange land, especially if your reputation and net worth are at risk. "When in Rome, do as the Romans do." If you don't like "Rome" or "Romans," look elsewhere for a business.

Gather data before worrying about price or financing.

Don't worry about price or financing before you collect and analyze all the relevant data about the business. It's easy to get sidetracked or abort a good deal if you focus too soon on what you think is a fatal flaw. Make note of it and then finish collecting data. When you have the complete picture, the benefits of the business may overcome its deficiencies.

Don't accept generic contracts from anyone.

Business purchase and sale agreements vary in complexity. Your attorney will show you the deficiencies in the generic buy/sell contracts, such as what is in use by some business brokers. There are several supplementary agreements that are necessary to make a safe, profitable investment.

Don't expect synergies to occur.

The potential for synergies can be the fool's gold too often during mergers and acquisitions. Often, they are not as valuable as people think they will be. And sometimes they do not arise at all. Acquisitions should be worthwhile, and priced accordingly, on the merits of the business for sale. Benefits arising from operational or financial synergies are a bonus.

Don't buy a declining company.

Except in extraordinary cases, revenue and profit in a tailspin usually ends in a crash.

Be careful if sales to one customer exceed 10%.

Do the math. A 10% reduction of the top line (revenue) usually ruins the bottom line (profit).

This is one of the first things business buyers, exit planning advisors and business brokers look for when they evaluate companies. Customer / revenue concentration is rarely a good way to run a business, especially if it exceeds 8%. Every customer whose revenue exceeds 8% is a risk to your business for if you lose one or more of these customers your company can instantly become insolvent. Expect to lose sleep if any customer's revenue exceeds 10%.

But, like most things pertaining to business buying, there is more to the story. Jeffrey D. Jones, on the topic of business valuation writes: "As an appraiser, the red flag is if any given customer represents 15% of total sales. Even then, it depends. How long have they had the customer? What is the relationship with this customer? Is the company one company or a division of a larger company that also does business with your company? Just a blanket statement not to buy if one customer represents 10% of total sales is too broad. I have sold businesses wherein one customer was 70% or more of the business. It does not mean the business is unsalable. It means the price will reflect this risk. Fair Market Value is a range concept. The higher the risk, the lower the price, but there will always be upper and lower limits."

Don't depend upon one product to sustain the company.

You can exponentially increase your probability for business buying success if you acquire a company that sells more than one product or service. You can do even better if one or more of the products are proprietary with a well-defined customer base (and the competitors know their place in the pecking order).

For an example of the problem with a single-product company, see our business buying don't, "Don't buy on a bubble." It refers to the low-carb diet craze. "To be sure, single-product companies are faring worse than their diversified packaged-food counterparts that also sell meat or dairy, such as agricultural giant ConAgra and Sara Lee. Sara Lee has meat, beverage, household products and apparel divisions in addition to its well-known bakery and dessert product line."

A long time ago investors had to go through expensive stock brokerage firms to buy or sell shares in publicly traded companies. That changed in a blink with the appearance of online transaction processors. For a few dollars, investors could instantly trade stock over the Internet. These processors did not offer advice; they simply handled trades. But that is changing. These single-product firms, which have proliferated to the point of saturating their industry with competitors, are looking for value-added services they can offer to customers for an incremental fee. It's the old story of businesses with foresight looking for competitive advantages. This is particularly important for transaction processors who only offer stock trading. They don't have the breadth of some of their competitors who operate in several other lines of business, such as brokerage advice, banking, or residential mortgages.

Timing is everything when buying into a fad.

Most buyers don't want to be left holding the bag when customer demand evaporates.

Here's another practical definition for "fad," from BusinessDictionary.com: "A desirable trend characterized with lots of enthusiasm and energy over a short period of time. Fads are often seen with common consumer items, especially around a holiday season. Products that have fallen into this category include Beanie Babies in the 1990s, and gaming systems in the 2000s. They can also be seen in other areas, such as investing. For example, leveraged buyouts (LBOs) were used frequently in the 1980s for companies looking to acquire rivals, suppliers, and other related entities. In the late 1990s, though, LBOs became less popular."

Don't buy if customers are changing buying habits.

First it was people you didn't know who were buying their medicines by mail-order from Canada. Then it was someone in your family. Now state and local governments and corporations are looking abroad for price discounts on prescription drugs. Owning (or buying) a neighborhood pharmacy in the U.S. is becoming increasingly risky.

Small photo labs provide another example. Technological advances (digital cameras) have forced these businesses to invest in expensive digital equipment so they can process their customers' conversion from film to digital images. One of these owners says, "I spent tens of thousands of dollars on equipment that became obsolete almost overnight. I had to scrap it for parts or sell it on eBay for a fraction of what I paid."

Levi Strauss & Co. may try to reduce its debt by selling its profitable Dockers brand, which accounts for about 25% of Levi's revenue. The firm says the sale should provide money to focus on making its jeans more appealing to fashion conscience consumers.

There are few instances where an entire industry is taken by surprise. The writing is usually on the wall long before adaptation becomes a do-or-die dilemma. Owners who keenly watch for changes and who have the courage to be one of the first to exploit change can position their company to grab market share from competitors. It's all about timing and action. The early bird can get the worm — but look carefully to be sure it *is* a worm and not a twig.

See a complete picture of customers.

Don't limit your customer investigation to sales. It's important to know who the customers are, their buying habits and the profit they generate for the firm that you might buy. But don't stop there. How do the customers use the company's products? This is not the same as asking about customer satisfaction. The use question is a window into why customers buy the product and what you can do to further serve their needs. Are there new uses that you see for the product?

Don't be afraid to ask customers: Why? Why not?

Why do they purchase products/services from the company that you might acquire? Price? Credit terms? Warranty? Right to return product? Quality? Service? Availability? Engineering? Can't elsewhere buy a comparable product/service?

Conduct your own market test, before buying.

It's common for first-time business buyers to be disappointed when the product or service doesn't sell or doesn't generate as much profit as they thought it would. Test the market for the product or service before you buy the business. (This requires the cooperation of the seller.)

To avoid wasting time and money on a business that may not be capable of generating the profit you require, it is important to prepare a written business plan with emphasis on the marketing part of the plan. With respect to marketing, it's not enough to know how present and former customers perceive their satisfaction with the business or its competitors. For your investment to be profitable, the business must make profitable sales to more customers. Large companies spend millions of dollars to find out whether people are going to buy their products and services. Although you cannot afford to spend too much money, you can conduct a test to learn more about market potential and what it takes to create satisfied customers. Here are some steps you can take:

Prepare a brief script to question customers about their satisfaction.

For those who say they will continue to buy from the company, ask what they think about its pricing. You are trying to learn whether you can increase prices or if there is pressure for a reduction. Everyone has a preconceived notion of what any product or service should cost, and regardless of the projected benefit, few will budge from this figure. Insist on a specific price.

Then ask: Is there any reason why you might not continue buying from us (or a competitor) in the same volume? You are trying to quantify sales volume.

Assuming you have gotten a favorable response, ask the customers how often (to learn about frequency of sales) they will purchase. Ask what is necessary for customers to buy more, sooner.

Inquire about competitor services that the customers use, have used, or have heard about. Determine their perception of those services.

After the interviews, summarize the responses.

When you have completed sampling the customers, sort the responses to determine the overall impression the market has of the company. The information will help you know, among other things: what you can realistically charge; when you can expect an order; financing or payment; the benefits customers expect; and the problems they perceive with the company.

After summarizing the responses, discard the most radical ones. The result will be an idea of how the target market generally will react to your sales effort shortly after you acquire the business.

Always try to test the potential of a product or service before you buy a business. Ask friends and family: Would you buy the product? How much would you pay? Run your own focus group, interview people at the local shopping mall—do whatever you can to get feedback on the marketability of the product or service.

Test your competitors' market demand, too.

Besides doing your own market test to evaluate a potential business acquisition, mystery shop your competition. It's easy. You or your surrogate pretend to be a prospective customer. Approach the company's competitors from various angles. Walk in, telephone, website, catalog, dealers, whatever. What you learn about their selling process and customer service will let you know what you will be up against if you buy the company. You will also pick up tips that you can use during due diligence, dealmaking and business planning. Want to know the identity of your soon-to-be competitors' key customers? Your surrogate, while shopping the competition, simply asks for references.

Don't ignore the reputations of key stakeholders.

Begin by asking the employees of the company for sale about the reputation and reliability of the company's key customers, employees, landlord, sources of financing and suppliers. Check online commentary about these stakeholders.

Don't neglect to evaluate viability of key customers.

To what degree is the marketplace changing in ways that can cause the company's top customers to lose *their* market share and hence adversely affect the buying power for what *your* target acquisition sells?

Don't confuse growth with profitability.

Just because a business can increase its revenue does not mean it will increase its profit. An increase in revenue generally relates to an increase in cost. Costs include cost of goods sold, overhead and cost of capital.

Don't fall prey to "he-said," "she-said."

It is common for people to buy a business or franchise without verifying the claims made by the seller. (More buyers have been hurt by seller omissions than by misrepresentations or false claims.) Your advisory team will show you how to document the seller's representations and warranties. Later, if the X$*T hits the proverbial fan, you will have recourse to mitigate your risk. If you can't prove your case, you might be out of luck, which might mean out of money and out of business.

Don't assume you can hold employees accountable.

You might not be able to hold the employees legally accountable for their misrepresentations about the company, which they made to you before your acquisition. Unless your purchase and sale agreement provide for it, you may not have any recourse against the seller after closing if you relied upon false or misleading information about the business provided by employees (or anyone besides the seller). Consider keeping a diary that recounts what people tell you, and ask the seller to confirm, correct or refute the information.

Don't let product trump profit.

Be careful about buying a business with insufficient profit because you are mesmerized by the business' product(s). If the owner can't earn a profit at or above the industry average for similar companies, why, exactly, do you think the company will do better under your ownership? If you make an emotional decision not supported by the facts, you will learn that "profit" is not a four-letter word, but "loss" is.

Don't like surprises?

I didn't think so. Don't rely on gut-checks. Check facts. Search for info about the person/firm on the Internet before you initiate a call to a business broker, seller, or potential business acquisition advisor. Do the same thing later during due diligence when you are investigating key employees, customers, suppliers, landlord, sources of financing. Forewarned is forearmed.

Good news is not the entire story.

All businesses have problems and face vulnerabilities. Most businesses can live with them until they solve or avoid them. When the seller finishes telling you about the bright future, ask him to illuminate the dark side.

Don't be hobbled by an inadequate financial system.

Rarely, in small and midsize companies, will you see a financial system that can help management ensure the business' deployment of resources for maximum benefit. But you should look for it (Don't expect it!) and know it when you see it.

During due diligence is an opportune time to begin envisioning ways to improve recordkeeping, accounting, and reporting methodologies, which you can implement post-closing. The most useful methodologies are simple and flexible. They help stabilize the company because they tell you what you need to know when you need to know it.

Adequate methodologies can avoid costly accounting, billing, payment, and other errors. A worthwhile system enables management to better understand their business, improve their ability to control costs and become more competitive in the marketplace. It can provide a data-driven basis for revenue and cost proposals, which can save valuable time and money. Decreased business risk is what you get with an adequate system.

Evaluate these components: accounting methodology, chart of accounts, budgeting and forecasting, financial analysis, the accounting and financial employees, and the company's service providers.

Don't expect or assume you will see accurate records.

It is common for the books and records of privately held businesses NOT to comply with generally accepted accounting principles. The business owner may not be trying to cheat anyone. Most owners keep their books in a way that is useful to the management of their business, which may not provide you with enough insight into the company to make informed decisions about it.

Important financial ratios to compute and compare.

Compute these and compare them to industry statistics.

LIQUIDITY RATIOS

It's not enough to focus on recent profit. Look for trends.

Current Ratio

- Reflects ability to meet near-term obligations. Too high a ratio can mean lost profits for excess liquidity.

- Too low invites cash crunch.

- Current Assets/Current Liabilities

Cash Flow Ratio

- If cash flow to total debt is less than 15%, expect a severe cash crunch. Add a low Current Ratio and disaster is around the corner!

- Cash Flow (Net Income + Depreciation - Cash Capital Outlays)/Total Debt

ASSET EFFICIENCY RATIOS

These ratios measure how well employed are the various assets of the business. The ratios provide insight into how to improve your return on investment.

Total Asset Turnover

- A measure of how well-managed the entire business is. If too high, the business is not generating the volume warranted by its level of investment. If too low, more investment could mean more profits.

- Net Sales/Total Assets

Inventory Turnover

- Frequency of converting inventory to cash or account receivable.

- Cost of Goods Sold/Average Inventory

Average Collection Period
- A/R Outstanding/Annual Net Credit Sales X 360

PROFITABILITY RATIOS

Compare to performance and alternative investments. Use *be-fore*-tax profit when comparing to other investments to eliminate the effect of taxation on those alternate investments. (Keep in mind that the basis of public company P/E multiples is *after*-tax profit.)

Net Profit Margin
- Reveals problems in marketing or cost control.

- Net Profit Before (or After) Tax/Sales

Return on Assets
- Net Profit Before (or After) Tax/Assets

Return on Equity
- Net Profit Before (or After) Tax/Equity

Don't be too focused on the financials.

By now, and by the time you finish reading *How to Buy the Right Business the Right Way—Dos, Don'ts & Profit Strategies*, you should realize that the financials are a small part of what you need to know to determine whether to buy a particular business. The company's relationships with its customers, employees, landlord, sources of financing and suppliers will determine the degree to which the company has more potential than vulnerabilities.

Verify required compliances.

Audit the company's compliance with labor, environmental and other requirements.

Don't blithely accept add-backs.

It is usual and customary for sellers and buyers to reconstruct the historical financial statements, so they more accurately reflect the performance of the business. However, do not accept the seller's add-backs at face value. Prudent buyers inquire into the validity of each add-back. Take depreciation, for example: Your cash flow budget should reflect what the business will spend to maintain or replace assets.

Don't overlook unfunded or contingent liabilities.

Unfunded and contingent liabilities mean cash crunches. Accrued vacation and other accrued paid time off can be a hidden liability. What is the value of it? Must it be paid in cash to terminating employees? Who will do the work, at what additional cost, when employees consume their benefit? What about underfunded or unfunded pension plans, warranties, and service contracts? Screen for these things early in your review of companies for sale.

Don't accept financial statements as-is.

Adjust historical financial statements to normalize profit and to reflect the actual value of assets and liabilities such as interest, owner compensation, add-backs of excessive owner perks, extraordinary/nonrecurring items, cash to accrual basis, inventory (LIFO to FIFO and quantity), employee accrued paid time off (an off-balance sheet item), and contingent liabilities. Depreciation is a special case. Analyze Section 179 deductions and capital investments.

"Earnings are commonly figured before depreciation. That's perfectly logical if the asset is real estate or something else that's not declining in value. But recognize depreciation if it is machinery and it's wearing out. It's a genuine cost of doing business." "Brokers for Hire," *INC. Magazine*

Anthony A. King, a lawyer with the firm of Minor & Brown, P.C. in Denver wrote this: "We recently represented an owner who did not appreciate the value of strong financial management. When approached by a prospective buyer (unbeknownst to us), our client provided his company's internal financial statements. Based upon these financial statements, the buyer prepared a draft letter of intent containing very specific purchase price adjustment parameters. Unfortunately, the seller's financial statements proved to be virtually worthless because they omitted important items such as long-term debt and incorrectly classified others such as shareholder notes receivable. When properly accounted for, these two items alone could reduce net worth of the company by 80 percent and result in a post-closing purchase price adjustment equivalent to 25 percent of the original price!"

Don't overly rely on the numbers.

The financial statements may accurately report what the company did, but were the firm's financial policies practical and legal? When was the most recent inventory of physical assets, and was the basis of the count sampling or complete? What about inventory obsolescence? What about actual and potential bad debts? What is the basis for depreciation for each asset? What is the financial forecast for capital expenditures, maintenance, and repairs? What about casualty losses? Is the company adequately insured? Are there pending changes in the terms of leases or loans?

Inadequate insurance increases your risk.

What about expensive insurance or insecure coverage (i.e., high probability of cancellation)? Evaluation of the risks that can be insured should occur before closing. If adequate insurance is not available and affordable, which you discover post-closing, you probably bought the wrong business.

Use the best kind of budgeting.

Zero-based budgeting.

According to investopedia.com: "Zero-based budgeting is a method of budgeting in which all expenses must be justified for each new period. Zero-based budgeting starts from a "zero base" and all the functions within an organization are analyzed for their needs and costs. Budgets are then built around what is needed for the upcoming period, regardless of whether the budget is higher or lower than the previous one. Zero-based budgeting allows top-level strategic goals to be implemented into the budgeting process by tying them to specific functional areas of the organization, where costs can be first grouped, then measured against previous results and current expectations."

Compute the break-even points.

Break-even point analysis is one of the most powerful tools to cut through smoke and mirrors. Using break-even point analysis will help you see the relationship between fixed and variable expenses. Using it forces you to identify the most relevant issues and then quantify them. With it, you can easily and accurately:

- Evaluate whether you can achieve the profit you want.

- Plan cost reductions.

- Examine expansion feasibility.

- Determine profit margins.

- Know how much cost can be incurred at no risk.

- Establish a selling price.

- Manage labor costs.

Prepare realistic cash flow forecasts.

Working with the seller, prepare a post-sale, after-tax monthly cash flow forecast for 24 months. This is the time during which you are most vulnerable. The owner may not be fully aware of the seasonality of his business, especially monthly negative cash flow.

Use the "justification for purchase" test.

This goes beyond your post-sale cash flow forecast. Besides making sure the business will not become insolvent because of the way you structure your purchase or the decisions you will make to manage it, the "justification for purchase" test also examines your return on investment, which includes the payback period (i.e., the amount of time it takes for you to recoup your investment in the business). Do this exercise before you sign a definitive purchase agreement or before you remove all the contingencies from the contract. This test helps you make a more realistic budget, and it will provide insight into the price, down payment, and other terms of purchase. Please don't be like buyers who say, "Don't confuse me with the facts."

Don't let someone else do your cash forecast.

Don't take the seller's word that his cash flow forecast accurately represents the future. If you don't do the cash forecast before you buy the business, you'll certainly do it afterward. The surprises will be all yours.

Be suspicious of "Seller's Discretionary Earnings."

What kinds of "earnings"?

Should it be pretax or after tax? What kinds of taxes?

Does the owner's and/or the company's income tax returns portray the profitability?

What about these commonly expressed representations of "benefit"?

- Adjusted Net Cash Flow

- Discretionary Cash Flow

- Seller's Discretionary Earnings

- Seller's Discretionary Cash Flow

- Owner's Discretionary Earnings

- Owner's Discretionary Cash Flow

- Company Annual Adjusted Net Cash Flow

All those phrases can be misleading. Very.

Did you notice the changing point of view in those titles? From "seller" to "owner" to "company"?

Now is a good time for you (i.e., the business buyer) to think about what the company's actual net cash flow will be, and the actual net profit, after you acquire the company.

Misunderstanding of it, and unfair manipulation of it, is a major reason why so many buyers do dumb deals.

Savvy buyers do not ignore the company's legitimate, ongoing expenses. They (maybe) ignore what was a one-time windfall profit or single-event catastrophic loss that will not appear again during the buyer's ownership of the company.

A company's actual net profit is what's left after the company pays the owner's reasonable salary and reasonable perks such as health insurance, automobile, and other expense allowances. (It's okay to add-back to profit excessive compensation.)

Adjusting the company's cash flow statement is done by adding back or deducting from reported annual net cash flow items such as:

- Income taxes

- Nonrecurring income and expense

- Depreciation and amortization

- Interest expense or income

- Total compensation for one owner/operator (assuming an owner works in the business).

It's a big mistake to treat these as though they are discretionary; they are not optional. Doing so means your company's net profit will be less than "Discretionary Earnings."

Keep in mind that a company's actual net profit is how the legitimate, competent business appraisers estimate value.

Make the kind of adjustments to income and expense that appraisers make.

Add back to net profit the excessive amount of owner's compensation. If interest expense or income won't continue after you buy the company, you might want to adjust the historical net profit. If you ignore depreciation, you better have cash available later to fund the replacement of assets. Ignoring depreciation also means you'll pay more than a company is worth; it's because of the inflated net profit upon which valuation models apply.

Be sure you understand the implications of adjusting the income statement versus the cash flow statement. Errors here mean a dumb deal.

Don't let sellers reclassify perks as profit.

As the owner of a business, you will have all the attendant headaches and risks. You deserve usual and customary perquisites, in addition to being paid the market rate to manage the business. Seller's discretionary cash flow should *not* include reasonable perks such as, health insurance, automobile, and other expense allowances.

Don't believe "discretionary" cash flow can pay debt.

Don't think "discretionary" cash flow is available to finance debt. Is owner's salary discretionary? Is health insurance? Is depreciation? Absolutely not. Treating these as though they are discretionary expenses is a big mistake. Doing so means you earn less than the business would spend to compensate a manager. It could cause the business to become insolvent and lead to a fraudulent conveyance, which puts your personal assets at greater risk. Use the business' net profit—after fair owner comp—to retire debt.

Don't assume the pension plan is properly funded.

The pension plan may not comply with the law and it may not be properly funded. Do not inadvertently allow the liability to shift to you after you buy the business.

Don't make a mountain out of a molehill.

Due diligence is to uncover problems and then devise a work-around for the most important ones. A *Business Buyer Advocate*'s job is not to be an impediment to your business acquisition. His goal is to facilitate the safe, profitable transfer of businesses—so every party to the transaction gets a win-win deal.

Franchises are not safer.

Franchises are NOT safer than independent businesses. Dealing with franchisors is rarely a pleasure; ask around about it. If you cannot effectively manage and finance a business, it will not matter whether you bought an independent establishment or a franchise (with its supposed support system).

"Look at the **darker side** of franchising before buying. While a tested business is safer than one started from scratch, the failure rate repeatedly touted by franchisors excludes stores that flop but are resold without closing. 'Probably at best a third are doing very well, a third are in definite trouble, and a third maybe break-even,'" says Rupert Barkoff, former chair of the American Bar Association's Forum on Franchising."

Require proof of franchises' "competitive advantage."

What exactly is the competitive advantage a franchisor has over other franchisors, and that its franchisees have over competing businesses? Test this by comparing the improvement in performance that exists between the franchise you are considering against other franchises and independent businesses. Items to test include: Market share; lower costs; higher profit; fewer failures; barriers to entry; a business that is more marketable when it's time to sell it (with the franchisor's conditions and permission, of course).

Compare franchises to non-franchises.

Buying an established non-franchise business might provide most of the perceived benefits that franchisors tout and not burden the business and its owner with franchising's restrictions, costs, and ongoing fees. It's advisable to include established, independent companies in your search.

In deciding whether to become a franchisee or to operate an independent business, compare what the seller of an independent business gives the buyer, during the buyer's transition into the company, to a what franchisors offer their franchisees.

- Compare the cost to hire employees or advisors to provide the assistance and expertise franchisors furnish.

- Compare the cost of inventory your franchise will purchase from the franchisor (or its approved vendors) to prices an independent business pays.

- The seller of a business and its employees and advisors train the buyer during the buyer's transition into the company. You're not starting from scratch.

- The seller of a business, for a limited amount of time, and the business' employees and advisors for a longer time, work for and assist the buyer.

- There is no evidence, which can be objectively verified, that a national affiliation makes a franchisee any more profitable or marketable (when it's time to sell the business) than a non-franchise business. It may be more difficult to sell a franchise for as high a multiple of earnings as an independent business.

- An existing business has an established name and established customers.

- Self-employment exists in an independent business.

- Starting a franchise can be faster than starting an independent, but purchasing an existing business bypasses the startup phase, which means you make money beginning the day you buy the established company.

- An existing, profitable company has a proven formula for success.

- An independent business has a perpetual life, unlike a franchise with a life set by the term of the franchise agreement. "Owning" a franchise is more like renting the business for the term of the franchise agreement.

A non-franchise business has benefits that are not available to franchisees: When you purchase an existing company, you don't add to the field of competitors, and you have total independence to operate the business any way you want and then sell it when you want on your own terms.

The bottom line is: *You* make your company successful or a failure, even with a top-rated franchise providing excellent support to franchisees.

Want a boss? Buy a franchise.

Go to the library. Read trade journals for any industry in which franchising is prevalent. You'll discover that some franchisable concepts breed more franchises. They compete with one another and everyone else in their niche. Their marketplace becomes saturated with competitors, so few make good money and some close.

Franchise owners who survive are stuck with a "job" they can't quit, and a "business" they can't sell.

Don't expect to buy an existing franchise with the hope of getting around the problems of starting one. If it's a winner, it's offered to existing franchisees or it becomes a company store. Don't be naive. Make inquiries.

Don't make this dangerous mistake with franchises.

Don't naively assume that it's wise to buy a franchise from a franchisor that passes your evaluation with flying colors.

- *After* a franchisor proves its capabilities, investigate the industry in which your business will operate, as if you were starting an independent business or buying an existing one.

Remember: Unless you buy an existing franchise location, you're starting a business; you're adding to the competition and the market share (pie slices) become smaller for most if not all the competitors!

Look for competition posed by franchises.

Avoid industries that are saturated with competing franchise systems.

Calculate the relative slices of the competitive pie.

Calculate the company's slice of the competitive pie, its market share. Do you want to own or compete with the big dog? Does the relative share of the pie excessively fluctuate? Do you want a small business that might be under the radar of bigger competitors? How easy/hard is it to gain and retain customer and employee loyalty? Is this important?

Don't presume you can get a bigger slice of pie.

Competitors put a limiter on your growth; when you push, they push back. The best and easiest way to grow is to serve an expanding quantity of customers. The next easiest way is to make more sales to your customers who themselves are getting larger. The toughest way to grow is to take away market share from your competitors.

"I have paid handsomely for business coaches who pushed for fast growth. We did everything they told us, the result being years of losses and debt. Now we've dialed back and become profitable again." "Slow and Steady," *FORTUNE Small Business*.

Franchising is not easy street.

When the former CEO of a major national franchise system, who has 20 years in the franchise business, bought a franchise, "he thought it was an ideal investment. If anybody should know, he figured, he should. As it turns out, he says he got fleeced. 'If I can fall for it, anyone can.' The 'franchisees' he spoke to had never owned franchises and the profits he had been promised never materialized. Charges of broken promises and hidden costs are just some of the numerous problems plaguing franchising today." "Franchise Fracas," *Business Week*.

How to steer clear of franchise financial disasters.

Zac Bissonnette, for *CNBC.com*, writes:

Investing in a marque franchise brand is no guarantee of success. Big national chains can get into trouble as easily as small independent businesses due to a wide range of missteps—from overexpansion to excessive debt.

Quiznos, the Denver-based sub chain with 1,600 locations in the U.S., filed for Chapter 11 bankruptcy protection. The same month Radio Shack announced plans to shut 20 percent of its 4,000 stores, including 900 that were operated as franchises.

Unfortunately, this is not unusual. History is littered with franchise companies that have hit the skids, including Dial-A-Mattress, Benningan's and Bally's Total Fitness.

- Know your franchisor's financial status.

- Check the franchise agreement for obligations.

- Look at the SBA loan default rate.

- Investigate the history of litigation.

Don't minimize the competition.

There are two types of competition. People who compete with you to buy businesses, and businesses that compete with each other. Failure to fully understand the degree of industry competition is the reason so many buyers regret their purchase. Industry consolidation is an insidious form of competition.

Here's what Gary R. Gerlach, Senior VP, George B. Hawkins has to say about it in his article, "What does industry consolidation mean for your company value?" Pick up the *Wall Street Journal* practically any day of the week and you will see an article on industry consolidation through mergers and acquisitions. Probably the most often used word when talking about mergers and acquisitions is synergy. The concept of synergy is simply that the sum of Company A's value and Company B's equals C, which is greater than the individual values of A and B. That is, 1+1 = 3. Two companies, combined, are worth more together than the two separately. Consolidators seek to purchase competitors in fragmented industries for a variety of reasons, including cost reduction by removing owner perquisites (e.g., owner compensation and benefits at levels higher than a professional management team) and eliminating duplicate distribution channels and sales forces, increasing profit margins by using increased volume to squeeze concessions out of suppliers, and buying access to new markets and new products. Also, consolidators believe they bring professional management skill to the table that is not possessed by the typical small, closely held business owner. Finally, consolidators may believe an entirely new business model is called for in an industry that stands to transform and reshape the landscape of how business is done. Keep abreast of the trends in the industry and look for those factors that indicate likely industry consolidation. Know who the consolidators in the industry are and what they are looking for in acquisition candidates. Most of all, when it comes time for a business valuation, rely upon a valuation firm that does not blindly use market acquisition data, but can analyze the company and the industry by those factors that generate value.

Don't overlook consolidation in customers' industries.

Industry consolidation among a business' customers can be dangerous. If the company you might buy serves numerous small customers and most of them come from the same industry, there is a good probability that, when they merge with *their* competitors, their larger purchasing power will enable them to extract concessions from your potential business acquisition. This may not be a bad thing. Instead of buying the type of company that might become threatened by consolidation among its customers, investigate buying one of the customers and then taking part in industry consolidation.

Don't ignore implications of changing trends.

Is this year's revenue or profit below the historical trend? Buyers must have good reasons to purchase a company with declining revenue, gross margin, or net profit. These are indicators of failure.

The social generational changes occurring over the recent decades has evolved from a work force willing to perform at its best into the "me" generation, which is much less committed to peak-performance and to their employers. Some industries, more than others, are affected by this. Keep in mind the shifting attitudinal culture while thinking about the kind of company you want to own, especially if your work ethic materially differs from a company's employees. Coping with them won't be easy.

Social and legal pressure and a declining unemployment rate is forcing up the minimum wage. Some companies are replacing fulltime workers with part-timers. Labor advocates are demanding, at the time this book is being written, a minimum wage nearly double the prevailing rate. Walmart, the largest private employer in the USA, is increasing wages for a half-million employees, a move that comes amid persistent scrutiny of its labor practices and high employee turnover.

Compute the power of economies of scale.

You may find a company for sale that is not what you seek. It may not be all that it could be. Let's say you find a small manufacturing firm, one with small competitors. Maybe this company could be a bridge to more opportunity. You could buy this company and then maximize the use of your factory. If the company, for example, is only running one shift, acquire (do not start) one or more of the small competitors who are barely making a profit. (If you go for a successful company, you will pay more than necessary to get the increase in revenue and profit you seek.) Shut down their premises. Relocate their assets to your shop. Schedule their employees onto your second and third shift. Use the cash you generate from selling the surplus equipment to pay down your business acquisition loan.

Don't buy big if it is more profitable to buy small.

The bigger the business the larger will be the multiple of profit used to price the company for sale. Think about a tactic in use by some of the top dealmakers. They buy several companies, one at a time over time, which individually are much smaller than they can afford. The pricing multiples are lower; the sellers are usually less knowledgeable about dealmaking. Combining these acquisitions or finding ways to profit from economies of scale can create a much bigger company, higher profit and more return on investment than is typical if you start buying the biggest company you can afford. "Roll-up" is a concept you can investigate.

Don't be blindsided by the competition.

It truly is too bad that so many business owners fail to observe what is going on. The airline industry, for example, is notorious for not caring about their customers. Airlines have intentionally ignored fundamental business rules, such as don't add more capacity than they can profitably serve. Some airlines have grown beyond the point where they can profitably support their size. Improvements are slow in coming, which creates an opportunity for competitors. Take JetBlue (among other discount airlines). These customer service and budget-conscious newbies have rattled the air travel business at the expense of the big boys, while providing considerable benefit to customers. This is the story of the little guy beating the big guy. It happens the other way, too. A recent headline proclaimed, "Department stores making a comeback." Less clutter and more exclusive merchandise propel sales to their highest level in 7 years. This in a climate of decreasing sales for many specialty retailers, most of which are small businesses. Need another example? Think Walmart and Home Depot.

Don't underestimate potential assault by competitors.

Failure to fully understand the degree of industry competition is the reason so many buyers regret their purchase. Industry consolidation is an insidious form of competition. If you don't detect an actual or pending assault during your diligence, before buying, your back will be against the wall the day you walk into your new business. It is usual for competitors to strike out whenever companies change hands. The new owner is busy coping with everyday issues, which exposes the company to assault.

Don't be blindsided by employees.

Some owners decide to sell their company upon learning that a key employee may quit and then compete with the company. Some sellers disclose this possibility to prospective business buyers. Buyers who take over a company with disgruntled employees start in second gear. The worst case we've seen happened to the buyer of a print shop. Within one month of the buyer taking over, the salesman, production manager and office manager quit. The new owner, who was a former corporate autocrat, had berated these employees, saying they were like sheep that needed his direction to accomplish anything. For payback with style, these people walked out the door for the last time wearing plastic sheep masks. They leased space across the street, so it was easy for customers to see the new competition. It took the buyer about one year to go out of business and then another year to wrap up his divorce.

Don't disregard employment regulations.

Are there any federal or state licenses, training, or education requirements that this business' employees must have? Do the employees comply? Will pending rule changes affect the company?

Avoid industries saturated with competitors.

Easy entry by startups can saturate an industry so the pie slices get smaller if the pie isn't growing. Similarly, capital intensive companies can saturate a marketplace. It is rarely wise to purchase a company in an industry saturated by competitors, especially if the company for sale does not have a commanding market share. One of the problems with franchises is they tend to multiply. You don't want to be in an industry where the quantity of businesses is growing more than the purchasing power of customers, because the slice of the pie gets smaller every time a new company enters the competition. Avoid industries saturated with competitors.

Identify recent cost increases.

When was the last time employees got a raise? Is the pay scale and benefit package up to par with what employees could earn elsewhere? Is a union organizer sniffing about? When was the last time suppliers raised their prices? What about insurance? (When you examine the cost of insurance, see if there has been a change in coverage or deductible.) If it's been a while, is it likely that the business' costs will rise after you buy it? If so, adjust the historical and future profit and then adjust your purchase price accordingly.

Identify revenue subject to adjustment.

What about the potential for accounts receivable bad debt? What is the exposure for sales that are subject to warranty or service claims?

Revenue fraud can cost you if you don't detect it.

It might not be intentional fraud. It could be improper revenue recognition practices. Either way, you need to know about it and do something about it.

Companies can use numerous methods to engage in premature or fictitious revenue recognition. Following are the most common techniques:

- Agreements / policies granting liberal return, refund, or exchange rights.

- Side agreements with customers and others.

- Channel stuffing.

- Early delivery of product.

  · Contracts with multiple deliverables.

  · Soft sales.

  · Partial shipments.

  · Upfront fees.

- Bill and hold transactions.

- Recording false sales to existing customers and false sales to fictitious customers.

- Round tripping.

- Other forms of improper recognition:

  · Recognizing revenue on disputed claims against customers.

  · Holding the books open past the end of a period.

  · Recognizing income on consignment sales or on products shipped for trial or evaluation purposes.

  · Improper accounting for construction contracts.

- Sham related-party transactions.

Source: "Common Financial Statement Fraud Schemes," Jamal Ahmad, JD., C.P.A., David Jansen, C.A., Jonny J. Frank, J.D., LL.M. Elaboration and other ways for fraud:

- Delivery of a product prior to customers' readiness to accept.

- Shipment of unfinished products

- Recognizing revenue before full performance has occurred under a contract requiring multiple deliverables.

- Backdating of agreements.

- Backordered sales.

- Recognizing revenue from installment sales prior to the appropriate period.

- Percentage of completion accounting.

- Misclassification of unusual, extraordinary, and nonrecurring gains as income from continuous operations.

- Over-accrual of rebates receivables due from vendors.

- Round-tripping, defined by businessdictionary.com as being a strategy used by businesses who sell an asset to another business with an agreement that the asset will be bought back at a time in the future. The strategy is used to increase the apparent amount of revenue and sales that have been made during a specific period. This practice is common in the business world but not everyone agrees it is a good business practice. Also known as round trip transactions.

Don't accept the books as-is.

It's a good idea toward the end of due diligence for your accountant to review the adequacy of the accounting system. This is not an audit; the purpose is to know the overall credibility and reliability of the business' accounting, reporting and financial controls. Are there accounting practices that have been too conservative, aggressive, or sloppy? What changes does your accountant recommend and what will it cost to make them? While your accountant is reviewing the records, ask her to verify that all the tax returns have been properly filed and taxes due have been paid. Have there been cutbacks in "discretionary" expenses such as advertising, personnel development, or maintenance?

Don't unquestionably accept accounting irregularities.

"Hewlett's Loss: A Folly Unfolds, by the Numbers," by Quentin Hardy and Michael J. De La Merced, *New York Times*, November 20, 2012: For Hewlett-Packard, the alarm bells started ringing less than a year after the technology company bought a British software maker for $11.1 billion. It was then that a senior finance official at the British company stepped forward, raising questions about the accuracy of the numbers. The problems complicate an already difficult turnaround effort.

Don't forget to anticipate resale value.

This topic comes from the article, *The 10 Main Do's and Don'ts When Buying a Franchise*, by ActionCOACH. What it says about franchises pertains to every kind of company.

"In the excitement of buying a business, it is important to remember to look toward the future. As the Swedish proverb says, 'the morning never knows what the afternoon has in store.' Even if the future of a franchise is bright, it still may be a good idea to sell it. In fact, if the outlook for a franchise is outstanding, that may be the most compelling reason to put it on the market and the best time to convert the business into a profitable sale while demand is high.

Before buying any investment, one smart piece of advice is to sit down first and figure out how to liquidate it. Knowing how to get out of an investment helps to figure out what the investment is worth, because it puts the buyer into the shoes of another buyer who may have a more critical eye. Changing the point of view can be a brilliant way to see a situation from a different angle and can help one think "outside the box" in an informative and innovative way."

Don't scare yourself silly.

How risky is it to own a company? Most business deaths are not failures. They are "voluntary dissolutions," according to Bruce Kirchoff, of the New Jersey Institute of Technology. In a study of 812,000 small companies, Kirchoff discovered that only 18% of them closed because of financial difficulties with creditors. Of those businesses that disappear, only 20% to 25% end up owing money to their creditors. In the study we learn about business failures by age. Of those who failed, it occurred like this: 1-5 years, 42%. 6-10 years, 25%. 10+ years, 33%.

Identify improvement opportunities, early.

Don't wait until after acquiring a company to identify improvements to the marketing plan. What you imagine will sell might not. Find out now what customers want.

Don't let your dream become your nightmare.

It feels good to pursue your dream of business ownership, which many consider to be the "American Dream." If you don't buy the wrong business or if you don't buy the right one the wrong way, your dream will *not* become your living nightmare. It is your advisory team that can make this possible.

Don't think the legal system will bail you out.

If you make a buying mistake, especially if you do so because of faulty due diligence and dealmaking, don't expect the courts to make you whole. You might not have enough proof to prevail, let alone enough cash for the battle. You could become broke before you can get a court date or collect on a judgment.

Don't be shortsighted.

Look way beyond the performance of the company and its industry. Understand the commitment to the business and the viability of its employees, customers, suppliers, landlord and sources of financing. What adversely affects them will affect you.

"Cement supplies drying up," was the headline of a news story. Cement producers could not keep up with customer demand because of mechanical problems at cement production plants. Moreover, a building boom increased demand. A contractor complained, after winning the bid for a job, "I was told it would be three weeks instead of three days for delivery. Recent price hikes for roof tile, drywall and other materials may increase my cost of materials up to 50%."

This story does not concern you, because you're not going to own a manufacturing business, right? In another headline, "Ice cream takes bigger scoop of cash," we learn about rising milk prices increasing the cost of ice cream. Pity the poor, small ice cream stores whose profit is being hard-hit by price increases "for just about every ingredient that goes into a sundae, from the ice cream to the cocoa and vanilla."

In an *AP* news report, we learn that Detroit automakers are at odds with their suppliers. U.S. auto parts suppliers are shifting their loyalties and resources to Japanese automakers at the expense of the Big Three, who generally treat suppliers as adversaries, according to a new study by Planning Perspectives, Inc. U.S. automakers repeatedly seek price reductions from their suppliers.

Are there phantom employees?

Are there family members or employees of another firm, which the seller owns, who work for the company you want to buy? The profit is overstated for your potential acquisition if they work without pay or if he or his other business pays them. Ask: How many people working for the business, even part-time, are not on the business' payroll?

Are there phantom vendors?

Are there vendors or service providers who work for the business that the business does not pay? Perhaps the business gets products or services that another company pays for. What about bartering relationships that are off the books and may not continue? The profit is overstated for your potential acquisition if the company gets anything without paying for it.

Don't underestimate the time it takes to buy a winner.

If you are under pressure to quickly purchase a business, you risk settling for a loser or dead-end business. If you cannot afford a buying mistake, begin the process with expert guidance. The typical amount of time to buy varies depending upon the type and size of company, the time of year and what you bring to the table. Your *Business Buyer Advocate* can interpret your situation.

Watch for these warning signs.

This will get you thinking:

Retail shops: Inadequate parking, short term lease, outdated inventory, excessive employee turnover, invasion by franchises, changing shopping habits (waiting for sales, switching to competitors).

Manufacturers: Recent incursion by or increase of competitors, dominance by one customer or supplier, changing technology, weakening industry from which customers come.

Any type of company: Numerous sellers, few buyers, declining industry.

Carefully review employee management.

If these functions exist, examine each one. If any are missing, ask why.

Employee handbook, job descriptions, fringe benefit program, new employee orientation and training, personnel records including performance reviews and contracts, etc.

Be realistic. Some if not all these items won't be documented for a small business. On the other hand, cope with all these issues. Make sure the owner explains them to you before you buy the company.

Don't readily accept alliances with competitors.

Some owners establish strategic alliances with "friendly" competitors. These can make it easier to manage the business. Some owners do this as a precursor to offering their business for sale, the idea being that the strategic partner might be the most probable purchaser. There is nothing inherently wrong with sleeping with the enemy. Let's say that Company A could serve a large, repeat customer but the specs for the product that the customer wants to purchase from Co. A is beyond the capability of Co. A to provide (at least initially). Company B competes with Co. A, but Co. B has the capability that Co. A is lacking. Companies A & B might decide to work together to serve the customer.

Sure, it's risky. On the other hand, the profit from a long-term relationship with the customer could be worth the joint venture.

Now back to you, the business buyer. Maybe the competitor had a chance to buy the business and chose not to do so. Perhaps Co. B knows something about Co. A that you need to know. Before you jump into bed with a competitor, ask your attorney if it is legal. Antitrust laws may apply.

Advertising and sales analysis are essential, early.

You can find bargains among faltering businesses if you are an advertising maven or are willing to hire one. If all else seems to be right with the business, but the owner does not know how to market its products/services, the business is probably dying on the vine. Are the customers of this type of business responsive to advertising? Is the business' spending on advertising much more or less than its competitors? Does it consistently advertise? What is the quality of the advertising, the other marketing activities and the techniques used to close sales? Ineffective advertising and salesmanship sabotage businesses. This can be good for a sharp and courageous business buyer.

Don't underestimate or overestimate the downside.

Buying a business is a major event. It will affect your lifestyle, emotions, relationships, and finances more than nearly any other investment. Don't be afraid of buying a business; be afraid of buying the right business the wrong way. Get advice without conflict-of-interest. Ignoring potential vulnerabilities invites trouble. What if revenue or net cash flow is less than you forecast? Have contingencies for the downside.

Don't confuse marketability with value.

What if too few buyers want to purchase the type of business you want to buy? You could pay a "fair" price only to discover that you can't sell your business. Marketability has to do with how much constant demand exists among business buyers for this type and quality of business. It also has to do with the economy. High interest rates, for example, can lower profitability and make it more difficult for buyers to arrange acquisition financing. Infiltration of an industry by franchises can repel buyers if the franchisees saturate the field with competitors.

Focus on what is and then what could be.

What you see may not be all you get (to pay for). Discover unrecorded and off-balance sheet liabilities. What about probable or pending litigation or governmental interference? What about the continuing cooperation of sources of financing? Check for secured debts; examine the Uniform Commercial Code filings.

"Local businesses oppose possible site for public transit station," headed a news report about the location of the station. This had been a topic of debate among various governmental and quasi-governmental agencies for several years. Owners, who joined the debate late, complained (but to no avail) about the potential threat to their business, which would occur during and after construction. (Three of the owners were recent business buyers.) Two years later, when the station opened, most of the nearby businesses were closed. The landlords were having trouble finding retail tenants. The wiser landlords are filing for a zoning change, from retail to office space. They hope to lease their buildings to the government, presumably so the government employees who thought it was such a good idea to locate the transit station in its present location could commute by public transit.

Skeletons in the closet?

- Has the company been the scene of a crime against anyone?

- Has the business been robbed, embezzled, or vandalized?

- Has the company had trouble with the governmental agencies?

- Is the company's location compliant with the zoning?

- What easements, exclusive rights or right of ways impact the business?

- Is company or its land hazardous with respect to governmental or other risks?

Look for off balance sheet and unrecorded liabilities.

What about potential liabilities? Potential litigation? Returns and warranties?

What about undiscovered, undervalued, and unpaid liabilities?

It is essential that sellers disclose to buyers, before closing, the degree to which work was performed without being compensated by the company (when, who, how much). Similarly, to what degree is there earned but unused paid time off such as vacation, sick time, etcetera?

What are liabilities? A company's legal debts or obligations that arise during business operations. Liabilities are settled over time through the transfer of economic benefits, including money, goods, and services.

Where is the risk with liabilities? Too many buyers too often don't detect all the liabilities and/or they don't recognize the value and risk of each kind of liability.

Actual liabilities are supposed to be reported on the company's Balance Sheet. What about actual liabilities that are not stated on the Balance Sheet, such as the employees' earned but unused paid time off (vacation, sick time, etc.)? Savvy buyers charge these to the seller (deducted from the purchase price and maybe reducing the down payment). What about accrued taxes, money due underfunded pension and other employee benefit plans, or rent and premise's occupancy costs associated with triple net leases? The allowance for bad debts?

Don't miss costs paid by another business.

Were all expenses relating to the business recorded? Have some of them been paid outside the business, perhaps by the owner or another of his businesses? Verify that the advertising and memberships that you know about are paid by the company, which you might buy and not another business. Likewise, equipment rental or leases, insurance, and various business services. What about professional fees or interest on loans? What about transportation or storage of goods? And don't forget business travel. In other words, don't take solace from the absence of usual and customary expenses.

Don't get soaked.

In another case, a DIY business buyer, too smart to hire a *Business Buyer Advocate*, purchased a large, new coin operated laundry. What he did not know until after he bought this "business" was that most of the thousands of condos and apartments surrounding the laundry had onsite washing machines and dryers. He also did not know that the main boulevard passing his shopping center would be closed for more than one year. The detour put vehicles on the opposite side of his location in the shopping center. The seller laughed all the way to the bank and is still chuckling while sipping Rum Runners on the beach.

Work with a safety net.

Many small business owners cross their fingers and hope catastrophe does not overcome them. Before you make an offer to buy a business, find out what types of insurance are available to cover the various risks that the business will encounter. It's scary enough to make a down payment from your savings and then to personally guarantee the business' financial obligations. It's downright careless to give potential litigants your blank check. It's not enough to have coverage for the perils you face.

Have sufficient coverage, as this story will illustrate. A business was sued and lost. The plaintiff's initial claim was for $10 million. The defendant's insurance policy provided up to $1 million of protection. The defendant lost at trial. The insurer paid $1 million of the $5 million judgment, which meant the business was hit for another $4 million. Makes the higher insurance premium for more coverage (which the business did not want to pay) seem cheap in comparison, doesn't it?

But that's not all. Employees don't like to work without a safety net either. It is becoming increasingly difficult for small businesses who "can't afford" to provide health insurance for employees (or subsidize the premium) to retain employees. These employees will quit to work for government or a larger business that can reduce their financial and medical risks.

Consider these types of insurance coverage: Casualty, public liability, Worker's Compensation, business interruption, motor vehicle, product liability, errors, and omissions (which might apply to your board of directors), plate glass, professional liability (if applicable), and employee medical.

Don't wing it.

Buyers who don't follow the optimum acquisition sequence can give the advantage to the seller. If you're having problems after buying, you might have jumped the gun, resulting in a post-closing mess. Sensibly progress through all the steps to find and buy a business. With our proprietary *Street-Smart 22-Step Acquisition Sequence* ™ which differentiates *Business Buyer Advocates* from typical professional service providers. Our methodologies can avoid pitfalls and keep buyers on track.

Don't omit the final walkthrough.

No matter how well everything is going before closing, make a final walkthrough inspection. Assets tend to disappear the night before closing. Verify the condition of the facility, records, equipment, and inventory. Your purchase offer should permit your final walk-through and it should have provisions to handle problems that arise. (Did you photograph or video the scene early in your dealmaking so you can compare then to now?)

See financial reports and tax returns. Consistency?

Reconcile the numbers. The seller won't provide the business' financial reports and tax returns? Be suspicious.

Discover the seller's promises to employees.

Is there an agreement between the owner and any employee that provides a benefit to the employee upon the sale of the business?

Don't presume employee loyalty.

Don't assume your perception or the seller's story is correct about the morale or loyalty of employees.

See the company's evaluations of key employees.

It is a sign of good management if employees are formally evaluated. Ask to see performance evaluations of key employees. You should know about the quality of key employees before you buy a business.

Don't finish due diligence without seeing resumes.

Examine each of the resumes as if you already own the company. Would you hire each key employee for each respective job description on the terms of their present employment? If not, why not? And what are you and the seller going to do about it?

Don't be blind to employees jumping ship.

Don't be deaf to complaining employees. Employees quit if the boss doesn't listen. Don't be blind to employees jumping ship.

During due diligence evaluate the roster of employees, paying particular attention to the reasons for turnover. And then, upon your arrival, post-acquisition, find out about employees that have been complaining to former management or among themselves. This can be a big problem if it is an indicator of coming events. When the company changes hands, employees don't know what to expect; some will expect the worst. Immediately neutralize their concern.

Don't make it easy for key employees to leave.

One of the best ways to retain the most valuable employees is for the company to enter into employment agreements with them. Make it worthwhile for them to stay with the company, and to perform on mutually agreeable terms. Paying a reasonable retention bonus or increasing pay or benefits may be less expensive than what it could cost to replace a key employee and train the replacement. And once you are in control, do not rush to upset the apple cart. Be sure and slow to change employee job descriptions or the routine ways the employees behave and interact with each other and with the company's customers and suppliers.

Question recent changes to job descriptions.

Employees' job descriptions/duties recently changing could spell trouble ahead. Some sellers reduce payroll, reassigning work to overworked employees before offering their business for sale. The temporary expense reduction increases "profit" and that causes uninformed buyers to pay more than the business is worth. The penalty for buyers doesn't stop there. It can be difficult to cope with disgruntled employees, with the best of them moving on to work for competitors.

Don't ignore changing perks.

It may signal problems ahead if employees' perks have been recently reduced. Ditto our explanation, above, regarding recently changing job descriptions/duties.

Red flags don't have to kill the deal.

Don't unnecessarily let red flags kill the deal if you can cut a better deal. Fixable vulnerabilities in the company provide you with opportunity to get concessions from the seller and then improve the business' profit after you buy it.

Know when to cut and run.

Your investment of time and money for dealmaking shouldn't prevent you from aborting a bad deal. It's better to take your loss, lick your wounds and then be smarter earlier during your next go at acquiring the right company the right way. Switching gears is a good time to evaluate the performance of your advisors.

Don't wait to learn the business until after you buy it.

On the job training is nice if you are an employee, but it is too risky if you are a business owner. If you are not expert in a line of business, study it (perhaps as an employee) before you buy into the industry. Learn the tricks of the trade before you buy so the tricks are not on you.

Remember your goals.

Before you proceed to pricing the business and dealmaking, ask yourself if the business provides the lifestyle and worklife you desire. What about its cash flow and profit? What about the potential to build your net worth?

Don't buy the company if the seller can't explain it.

Don't let the intentionally "blind" make you disabled. Sellers, for example, who say they do not know, or they pretend not to know the business' numbers can derail you if you do not cause them to thoroughly and accurately document what you and they need to know about the historical and near-term future of the company.

Don't buy the company if you can't explain it.

The seller has convinced you about the wonderful benefits of his business. What if you have trouble explaining your rationale for wanting to buy it when you talk to your advisors, friends, and family? If they don't buy your story, maybe you should not buy the business.

Don't overlook how you will create liquidity.

Keep in mind while you are evaluating the business how you will create liquidity. After buying the firm, you might want to convert part of your ownership stake into cash by selling a partial interest to a key employee, for example. The business itself might need more cash than it usually generates. What exactly will you do to create more liquidity and how long will it take before it occurs?

Don't buy it unless you know there are other buyers.

A business worth buying is one that other buyers will want to purchase from you when it's time to sell. Don't wait until after you buy to determine whether you made a good buy or that you won't be able to say goodbye without going out of business.

How, exactly, will you better- manage the company?

Sometimes it is a good idea to base your decision to buy a company on "what you see is what you get" instead of "I can do better than the present owner."

Ask the catch-all question.

Ask the seller these questions: Do you have knowledge of anything within your company, its industry or your marketplace that may adversely affect the viability and/or profit of your business—or a buyer's decision to purchase it? You might follow up with more questions: Is there any revenue or expense relating to your business that does not appear on its financial statements? Is your company in default on any of its contractual, warranty, financial, taxation or other obligations?

Don't forget the most important questions.

What are the competitive advantages of this company? What are the dependable drivers that create customer demand for its product? From these questions will come many others. Follow the string to its end to discover the truth about the business. Do this before buying.

What are the elements of "competitive advantage"? Everyone seems to know what it is, yet few can articulate it.

Definition: Competitive advantage exists when a business' profit and reputation is above the norm for its industry. It occurs when the business is more capable than its competitors of managing the resources available to it.

Warren Buffett says the most important thing he looks for when evaluating a company is its "sustainable competitive advantage."

A business does not earn a true competitive advantage because of a windfall or a lucky year. Its advantages must be sustainable. This is what separates the good businesses from the superior ones.

But knowing the definition is not enough, is it? It's useful to identify the resources and the variables which, when efficiently managed, create each competitive advantage.

Competitive advantage is comprised of the strength of a business' position in its marketplace (because of its brand, human resources, dominant products, etc.); its superior degree of growth in relation to its competitors; the quality of its products, location and management; its ability to acquire capital; the effectiveness of its strategic planning; its profitability above the industry average; the longevity of its products in comparison to its competition; the variety of its product line and the introduction of new and/or improved products; its synergies from internal processes or alliances with other organizations; economies of scale; and lower costs, perhaps because it controls its source(s) of supply.

Tip: You cannot define a business' competitive advantage in a vacuum. Understand your competitors' business because a company's advantages are in the context of its industry.

"Operational effectiveness means performing similar activities better than rivals perform them, whereas strategic positioning means performing different activities from rivals' or performing similar activities in different ways. Few companies have competed successfully on the basis of operational effectiveness over an extended period." "What Is Strategy?" Professor Michael Porter, *Harvard Business Review.*

Peter Ebner, a marketing consultant in Ontario, Canada, asks this: "What is your company's most valuable asset? When answering this question, try to be specific. Don't just say, "It is my equipment, location, inventory and employees."

Require the seller to promptly notify you of changes.

Don't forget to require the seller to promptly notify you about material changes occurring during your evaluation of the company . . . right up to closing.

A company blindsided by the loss of an important customer, or something that can adversely affect the premises lease or access to the business' location, or a lawsuit or governmental regulatory notice of infraction are examples of what you must know so you can decide whether to continue dealmaking or abort the deal.

CHAPTER 5

Pricing / Valuing the Company

"Accurately valuing a small business is often the most challenging part of the process for prospective business buyers. However, it doesn't have to be an overwhelming or difficult undertaking. Above all, you should realize that valuation is an art, not a science. As a buyer, always keep in mind that the "Asking Price" is NOT the purchase price. Quite often it does not even remotely represent what the business is truly worth," writes Richard Parker, president of The Business for Sale Buyer Resource Center™.

This chapter shows how to do it, so you can avoid pitfalls along the way.

Indication of value begins with this.

"Indication of value?" is a FAQ from searchers screening sellers of SMBs. Keeping in mind that there's a huge difference between value and price, below is the minimum I need to begin assessing the fair range of pricing, from the buyer's view.

I advise searchers to run, not walk, away from brokers/sellers who don't, upfront, provide this info in a reliable format.

Completion of my form to score the company's *nonfinancial* factors. It helps us compute the risk multiple that we apply to the business' "profit" (or whatever is the relevant indicator).

- It is IMPOSSIBLE to value a business without understanding the nonfinancials.

Plus the seller's . . .

- Assertion for the financial "value" for all the assets (including inventory and goodwill, stated separately) to be conveyed to the buyer at closing.

- Pretax net profit for the trailing 36 months.

- Asking price and terms.

- Amount of seller financing.

- Amount of necessary working capital.

Return ON and/or OF investment.

Don't get caught holding the bag. This may surprise some of you. Return *on* Investment is not enough. I've seen countless buyers of SMBs wish they hadn't done the deal when they discover they merely get a return on their investment . . . but they could not get the return *of* their investment.

It's not a good idea to buy a business that you can't sell when you want to exit.

Don't ignore this truism.

Buyers suffer because they ignore this truism: You can pay too much for a good business, but you can't pay too little for a lousy one. The problems we feature in this book stem from defective acquisition techniques, not a lack of good businesses. Every year, thousands of business buyers buy the right business the right way. But other buyers wish they had not purchased a business, because they bought the wrong business or the right business the wrong way.

I have never cared what something costs; **I care what it's worth.**

— Ari Emanuel

Don't overpay.

Buyers beware. It is common for a business owner to erroneously price his business at 2 to 5 times recast cash flow. Valuation rules-of-thumb are not reliable and do not comply with IRS pricing formulas. When recasting profit, do not exclude from expense the owner's pay and perks or depreciation and interest.

On the other hand: Overpaying may be right for you.

Don't think the seller or your advisors KNOW what a business is worth to YOU.

I struggle to write this but sometimes it is a good business decision to "overpay" for a worthwhile business, to get control of it, if doing so takes you where you want to go, and if the company's profit can pay the entire price plus the acquisition financing costs and the additional cash investment you deposit into the company concurrent with purchasing it.

Of course, before you can "overpay" you must know what a reasonable buyer would readily pay for it. This is your floor price if you must prematurely sell it.

Don't be embarrassed by valuation dysfunction.

Valuation inadequacies are common. You could be in big trouble if you did not obtain a credible, third party opinion of value upon which you relied when making your purchase offer. This is so obvious that, here, I won't discuss it. Instead let's look at some of the elements of value.

Just about everyone is aware of the need to consider depreciation when valuing assets, such as physical wear and tear and economic obsolescence. But some people don't pay sufficient attention to functional obsolescence; in other words, do the assets perform the job as intended? If not, what's the penalty if not updated or what's the cost to update?

To some business valuators (such as me), valuing the anticipated stream of company net profit is as, if not more, important than valuing the assets and liabilities. After all, assets and liabilities are nothing more than the means to generate the profit. The starting point to value the historical and anticipated stream of net profit is the financial return on investment the buyer requires in return for purchasing a company. That figure rises and falls because of the buyer's perception of risk for each potential acquisition.

Do you know enough about business valuation?

Read the IRS Revenue Ruling 59-60 and its updates. It is the fundamental standard for valuation. It explains numerous approaches to value. None of the methods work alone. An appraiser correlates them to reach a conclusion about value.

Don't confuse value with price.

Value, theoretically, is the amount at which a business changes hands between a willing seller and buyer when the seller is not under any compulsion to sell and the buyer is not under any compulsion to buy, both parties having knowledge of relevant facts. A smart seller knows how to get the buyer to *want* to pay the highest price by creating buyer competition and showing the business in its best light. A professional business valuation is the irrefutable remedy when sellers, brokers or buyers disagree on price.

Long ago, Ben Graham taught me:
"Price is what you pay; value is what you get."

— Warren Buffett

The asking price rarely has anything to do with value.

The seller's asking price is not the benchmark from which a wise business buyer makes an offer to purchase. Successful business buyers make their initial offer from the perspective of an independent, competent business valuation.

Don't be scared away if the asking price seems too high.

It's not necessarily a problem if the seller's asking price is higher than your initial opinion. It is not worth losing what could be a profitable acquisition or merger, which can happen if you prematurely argue with the seller or broker about price. During due diligence the most reasonable selling price should become apparent to you, and then you can explain your rationale to the seller. If, however, the asking price is much greater than you think it should be, simply ask the seller or broker to explain the rationale. If you believe it, you can negotiate later. If not, abort the deal.

Don't rely on valuation rules-of-thumb.

Rule of thumb or rule for the dumb? Don't rely on valuation rules-of-thumb.

The only reliable rule of thumb is there are no reliable rules-of-thumb to value a business. Buying a business, for most people, is the largest and riskiest financial decision of their life. Get a *Price Fairness Opinion* before you make an offer to purchase.

"A rule of thumb is a homemade recipe for making a guess. It is an easy to remember guide that falls somewhere between a mathematical formula and a shot in the dark." Tom Parker, Business Broker.

"Critics of rules-of-thumb claim that a rule is simply an average and doesn't allow for the variables of each individual business." *Tom West,* Business Brokerage Press.

"Rules-of-thumb and multipliers don't work; they disregard profit." *The Complete Guide to Buying and Selling a Business,* Arnold Goldstein.

"So-called industry multiples and rules-of-thumb are a poor substitute for a properly performed market price evaluation. They are generally not reliable and oftentimes indicate a value that bears no relationship to the actual market value of the company." *American Business Group, Mid-market Merger & Acquisition Letter.*

Don't omit factors affecting value.

The basis for a business' value is its profit and its potential. Its potential is influenced by many factors some of which are: Type, size, and momentum of the business; its competitive position; the demand by business buyers for this type/size of business; the risk that all businesses in the industry face; the relationship between the business and its customers, employees, suppliers, landlord and sources of financing. Don't forget one of the strongest forces—the motivation of the business owner to sell versus the buyer's desire to purchase the business.

Your capabilities can add to the business' potential for efficiency and/or growth, but don't tell the seller about this.

Jeff Jones, president of Certified Business Appraisers Inc. and chairman of Certified Business Brokers, Houston, TX says this: Risk factors are what make one business different than another. Three key risk factors are: depth of management, diversity of products or services and geographic dispersion. Does all the company's critical knowledge reside in only one or a few people? How narrow is your marketplace?

Using one or too few valuation formulas is risky.

There are at least nine valuation methods that are generally used by professional business appraisers. These techniques are encouraged by the IRS, courts, and lenders. Don't fall for the myth of an average price.

Toby Tatum is a longstanding business appraiser and business broker. He writes in his article, "Why some businesses sell above median value," I can think of five reasons to explain why some businesses trade well above the median value. The first, and probably the most predominant one, being the terms involved in the transaction; next, some buyers just pay too much for the business; some of the transactions reported as trading at extremely high P/E multiples probably included the sale of real estate owned by the business in addition to the business itself; some transactions include an earnout provision. I think the preceding four reasons provide a good explanation for most of the transactions trading at the high end of the continuum. However, there is one other explanation for very high P/E ratio transactions I have read about. That is the fraudulent buyer who has no intention of consummating the transaction in good faith. Such an individual is not really a buyer at all but a con artist posing as a buyer. The scam the business-buying con artist practices is known as a "bust-out." The key to success in this scam is to induce the seller to finance most of the purchase. Typically, the trick used to lure a seller into the trap is to consummate the transaction at a price far above any reasonable value for the business—i.e., to appeal to the seller's greed. Such a commitment means nothing to the buyer because there is no intention of ever paying the balance of the purchase price.

"Once in control, the buyer does everything necessary to increase the near-term cash flow such as stretching accounts payable, giving deep discounts for cash purchases, defaulting on lease payments or note payments, insurance premiums, and so forth. This is compounded by selling fixed assets not immediately needed (sometimes just for scrap value), borrowing cash if possible and essentially doing anything else that will generate cash. And finally, just before disappearing, stiffing employees on their paychecks. How much time does it take to accomplish all this mayhem? About one month." (This last reason is a quotation from my book, *How to Get ALL the Money You Want For Your Business Without Stealing It* ™.)

Don't misunderstand pricing multiples.

Nearly every business in nearly every industry sells for a narrow range of a multiple of net profit. Know the full range; do not use an average. Some of the best deals are priced at the top of the reasonable range of value. So are some of the worst deals!

Don't permit these valuation errors.

There are too many errors during valuation to cite here. Do-it-yourselfers should shy away from business appraisal.

Errors can arise due to these things (in alphabetical order):

- adjustment of historical financial statements

- inappropriate market risk discount or premium

- miscalculation or omission of performance ratios

- comparing private companies to public companies

- extrapolation of historical data into the future

- failure to recognize that value perception is heavily influenced by the expected return on investment and the risk assessment for each seller and each particular buyer

- improper inclusion of non-operating assets

- inappropriate risk-free rate for the valuation

- interpretation of cyclical or seasonal companies

- interpretation of economic conditions

- key person discount

- marketability of the business for sale

- misjudgment of liquidity risk

- misunderstanding goodwill

- neglecting to value intangibles

- nonsensical relationship between discount rates, return on investment and economic inflation or deflation

- reproduction cost

- residual value at end of projection period

- special interest purchaser

- focus on financial but not non-financial factors

- use of pricing multiples and rules-of-thumb

- weighted average cost of capital (WACC)

- wrong calculation of net cash flow

Last but not least:

- Confusing value with price.

Don't rely on a seller's valuation.

A business buyer is at a disadvantage if s/he relies on or rejects an appraisal that a seller purchased. Wise buyers order a valuation from a credible, independent third party.

Don't rely on a broker's valuation.

You asked for it; you got it. You deserve its consequences. It's not a good idea to rely on the opinion of value expressed by the seller's broker.

Asking prices are the starting point. It is the height of stupidity to rely upon an opinion of value from anyone that has a conflict-of-interest.

As soon as you know (post-acquisition) you've been snookered as to the price you paid, find out what other buyers would pay, right now, were you to offer your company for sale.

Don't be misled by "advisors."

There are numerous wolves in sheep's clothing looking to fleece the unsuspecting business buyer. Conflict-of-interest and easy-to-digest platitudes are the common denominator among them. Charlatan is an apt label in some cases. These advisors provide their dangerous insight through the Internet, publications and/or personal counsel.

Below is an example from an "advisor" to business buyers. We paraphrase (so we don't have to identify the source).

- Don't waste time or money getting a professional valuation. Let the seller do that. There are very good, inexpensive software packages available that will do the same thing at a fraction of the cost. Valuations are not scientifically based; they're subjective. Valuation is a personal formula: What's the business worth to YOU?

Duh, if "valuations are not scientifically" (objectively) based, then they are subjective. Informed people know that computer software cannot handle all the subjective variables unique to every industry and then reliably price a business.

Business buying is not like home buying.

The selling price of houses is a public record, which is easily accessible by anyone. It is nearly impossible, without going through a service provider, for a business buyer to get reliable statistics from independent sources that report comparable business sales and the terms of the sales. It is much easier to compare the features of a house than it is to compare businesses. If you buy a house that you don't like, you can sell it. You cannot quickly sell a business if it becomes your don't-wanter.

Don't rely on hearsay.

The negotiated terms of purchase contracts are hush-hush for most privately held company buy/sell transactions. Business appraisers have access to company sale statistics. The identity of businesses is concealed in various national done-deal databases. Comparative data includes:

- Quantity of similar businesses sold.

- Business type.

- Standard Industrial Classification for the business sold.

- Location.

- Annual revenue of businesses sold.

- Annual earnings before owner's comp, interest, and taxes.

- Owner's compensation.

- Sale Price: Total consideration.

- Price/Gross Ratio: Total consideration/annual gross revenue.

- Price/Earnings Ratio: Total consideration/annual profit.

- Year & month transaction consummated.

Don't assume similar businesses are alike.

For example, if two U.S. manufacturers produce the same kind of product and one of the companies sells to the U.S. government, that company may be prohibited from including foreign materials in the product. Look into the Buy American Recovery Act. It provides that, unless one of three listed exceptions applies (non-availability, unreasonable cost, and inconsistent with the public interest), and a waiver is granted, none of the funds appropriated or otherwise made available by the Act may be used for a project for the construction, alteration, maintenance or repair of a public building or public work unless all the iron, steel and manufactured goods used are produced in the United States.

Detect inventory frauds.

These are some of the inventory frauds seen by Suren Rajakarier, KPMG:

- Failing to write down obsolete inventory results in overstated assets.

- Mismatching of cost of goods sold with revenues.

- Manipulation of the physical inventory count, inflating the unit costs used to value inventory. Companies have even made pallets of inventory with hollow centers,

- Placed bricks/sand in sealed boxes instead of high value products.

- Companies have even programmed special computer reports of inventory for auditors that incorrectly add up the line items to inflate the overall inventory balance.

- "Bill and hold" items, which have already been recorded as sales, might be included in the physical inventory count, as might goods owned by third parties but held by the company on consignment or for storage.

- Large value of inventory in transit is created, in a place where it is hard for auditors to observe it.

- Shuttle inventory between locations being observed by auditors on different days, to double count the inventory.

Properly value inventory.

Don't improperly value assets, and in the case of inventory is it too little, too much, obsolete? The savviest buyers hire independent, credible (without conflict-of-interest) specialists to value inventory and other assets. Naïve buyers misunderstand the effect of obsolesce and depreciation; they believe the company's' Balance Sheet.

Focus on more than tangible assets.

Tangible assets are important, but the value of a business is influenced more by its intangibles such as goodwill. Make a mistake valuing a tangible asset and you pay more than it is worth. Overvalue goodwill and you make a bad investment.

An appraisal is about more than "value."

What's it worth? This is just one thing a competent business valuation will tell you. A business appraisal provides the reasonable range of value from which you negotiate your purchase price. But that's not all. You will learn about the relative marketability of the company (i.e., feature and benefits, risks, and vulnerabilities that attract/repel buyers). You will get a second opinion about your due diligence. You will see the business and its industry in a new light because of your appraiser's perspective. You might get a wakeup call if the report zeroes in on something you were apt to minimize in your zeal to buy the firm.

A good appraisal is a wonderful tool to use with family members who are not as excited about buying a business as you are. You'll have a leg up if (gasp!) the IRS decides to audit your acquisition. You can use the authoritative power of an expert third-party to explain your purchase offer to the seller.

Identify and value intellectual property.

Are you enjoying this book? It's an example of intellectual property. Make sure you investigate the protection companies have for their patents, trademarks, trade names, copyrights, and license agreements. Do these protections transfer to you when you buy the company?

According to attorney Michael J. Dunne: The concern for intellectual property due diligence cannot be limited to high-tech businesses. Almost any business is reliant to some extent on technology and its ability to use and leverage its rights to such technology. The more important the technology to the entity's core business, the greater the focus which should be placed on intellectual property due diligence, even when the acquisition or other transaction is not being made expressly for the purposes of acquiring such technology. If the technology is protected as a trade secret, the acquirer will need to investigate the efforts taken by the target to follow appropriate confidentiality practices. And while various techniques may be used to protect an acquirer after the deal closes (such as holdbacks in the purchase price and indemnification from the target or the target's principal shareholders), the best protection often turns out to be learning as much as possible before closing.

Don't fall for blue sky schemes.

Blue sky goes by other names, such as goodwill, potential, not grounded, unrealistic, impractical and without immediate commercial value. Especially in estimating something such as the worthiness of a company and its value for a new owner.

According to the BusinessDictionary.com: "Largely speculative venture which promises huge returns but is also highly risky. The name comes from the comments of a Kansas state (USA) Supreme Court judge that such schemes have no more basis than 'so many feet of blue sky.'"

Therefore, if you will be materially responsible for improving the company and for making it more profitable than it has been under the present owner and management, don't pay the seller for what you will bring to the table. Pay for what the business has earned. (Alternately, see "earnout" in this book.)

Gaze at blue sky; don't buy it.

According to one of the most renowned and longstanding business appraisers, **Shannon Pratt**, "If a sale goes through at an exaggerated price, it can boomerang against the seller in seller-financed transactions. Buyers who are overburdened with debt tend to default, dumping the company back on the seller's lap. A large proportion of these are never paid off."

Shannon Pratt continues: "Many brokers disregard the common-sense notion that cash flow should be net of reasonable owner compensation, and that cash flow should be adjusted to reflect any improvements or capital expenditures that will be needed in the future to maintain the current earnings stream."

Brokers confuse goodwill with blue sky. Goodwill is supported by the historical earning capacity of the company. On the other hand, blue sky is projected future earnings based upon assumptions that are not supported by the company's historical performance. Buyers will seldom pay for blue sky, but they will buy goodwill. The difference between the two is cash flow. *American Business Group/ Mid-market Merger & Acquisition Letter*

If the seller's or broker's representations paint an exaggerated picture of the company's future, and it turns out that the buyer relied on them in reaching his decision to purchase the company, there could be costly legal consequences. *Robert Machiz, American Business Group*

Don't assume that the business has goodwill.

The IRS defines goodwill as the difference between the selling price of a business and the value of the "tangible" assets that buyers purchase. When sellers cannot present buyers with a credible rationale for the value of the business' goodwill, buyers call it blue sky. Then the argument begins.

The basis of goodwill is the company's historical profit. It has to do with the commercial advantage the company has over its competition—because of its location, reputation and relationship with its customers, employees, landlord, lender, and suppliers.

Here are some of the issues that business appraisers consider when valuing goodwill: Is the continuity of income at risk? To what extent is the marketplace competitive and stable? To what extent is the business' revenue cyclical or seasonal? Is the business growing slower or faster than the industry average? To what extent do nonfinancial factors cloud the business' future? In what phase of a business life cycle is the firm? What is the relative demand by business buyers for this type of business in comparison to other types of businesses for sale?

Don't let goodwill mask ill will.

It's good to buy a company with goodwill. But look for ill will, too. Negative experiences with the business, especially recent events, suffered by competitors, customers, employees, suppliers, sources of financing, governmental agencies or the landlord can generate anger and a desire for retribution. Gently probe for ill-will and rumors when you interview people who interact with the company.

Don't conflate goodwill with good luck.

Goodwill or good luck?

The IRS defines goodwill as the difference between the selling price of a business and the value of the tangible assets that buyers purchase.

Beware of goodwill, especially if its basis is the owner's personal relationship with the company's C.E.L.B.S. ™. To what degree can you reasonably expect to match or surpass the quality of the seller's business relationships with the company's customers, employees, landlord, bank, and suppliers?

Meaningful transitional assistance by the former owner for the buyer is especially important if the "value" of goodwill is a significant part of the purchase price. If the acquisition turns out to be a dumb deal, the company won't have enough assets to generate enough money if the business is liquidated. And trying to seek recourse from the seller may be like squeezing blood from a turnip. The sad truth is too many buyers suffer lousy transitional assistance. Therefore, let's, concentrate on goodwill instead of good luck.

Perspective: "In the final analysis, goodwill is based upon earning capacity. The presence of goodwill and its value, therefore, rests upon the *excess* of net earnings over and above a fair return on the net tangible assets." *IRS Revenue Ruling 59-60*

Don't assume the business has goodwill. When sellers cannot present buyers with a credible rationale for the value of the business' goodwill, savvy buyers call it blue sky. Then the argument begins. Don't let goodwill mask ill will.

Buyers may pay for goodwill if sellers demonstrate, because of the business' commercial advantages and its unique competitive advantages, that it can generate a profit *above* a reasonable return on the business' assets. Factors to consider include its management, trade secrets, location, reputation, profit compared to its industry average, degree of barrier to entry, proprietary technology, and the quality of relationships with and the capabilities of its customers, employees, landlord, bank, suppliers.

Don't think "profit" means profit.

Most people define profit as the excess of revenue over expense during a particular period. It's not that simple. Business owners want their financial investment in their business to provide a return commensurate with its risk. Therefore, the surplus of revenue over expense is reduced by the monetary return on investment that an owner expects. Let's say you pay cash for a business. The price is $5,000,000 and 10% ($500,000) is the minimum annual ROI that you expect. If the business' surplus of revenue over expense (commonly referred to as "profit") is $1,250,000, $500,000 of this provides your minimum ROI. The remainder, $750,000, is known as "excess earnings." Excess earnings consider the cost of money.

Businesses with excess earnings enjoy a higher valuation because they generate a return on *and* of investment *while* you own it. A business that has excess earnings has goodwill as part of its value.

If you don't sell a business with excess earnings until it recoups your investment and pays the annual ROI you seek, whatever you sell it for is a lucrative windfall.

A business can suffer negative excess earnings. This is not good. When this occurs, the business may not be marketable (to a knowledgeable buyer) as a going concern; it may be worth no more than the value of its tangible assets. In some cases, liquidation value is all that one can expect from it.

Don't use book value or the seller's estimate of FMV.

Obtain a third-party appraisal of value from which to discuss price if you and the seller cannot agree on the current fair market value of the (used) in-place assets.

Don't misadjust financial statements.

Buyers should beware of adjusting or recasting revenue, expenses, capital expenditures and net cash flow. Adjusting / recasting the financial statements (aka "normalizing") poses extreme risk for buyers that rely on help from anyone shouldering conflict-of-interest.

According to one of the most renowned and longstanding business appraisers, Shannon Pratt, "There's a tendency to take off things that ought not to be taken off, primarily a reasonable salary for the owner. That's not profit."

Depreciation is too often improperly "normalized." According to an article in *INC. Magazine*, "earnings are commonly figured before depreciation. That's perfectly logical if the asset is real estate or something else that's not declining in value. But if it is company machinery and it's wearing out, you should recognize that depreciation. It's a genuine cost of doing business." Shannon Pratt writes, "Depreciated replacement cost is the current replacement cost reduced by the percentage of useful life that the existing assets have been in service."

Make relevant adjustments to the financial statements.

Adjustments to the financial statements are necessary to perform a realistic valuation and to reasonably price the company for sale or purchase.

Financial statements are the basis for valuing a business. Substantial errors may result if you do not adjust earning power (Income Statement)—as follows:

1. In the way your firm elects to account for its activities.

2. To discount/eliminate past events that will not recur.

3. To handle discretionary items.

On the Balance Sheet, asset values usually need adjustment. They may affect the Income Statement. 8 of the most typical 17 items follow:

- Allowance for bad debts

- Pension liabilities

- Employee vacation time earned

- Depreciation methods

- Capitalization versus expensing

- Nonoperating/nonrecurring items

- Transactions with owner(s)

- Asset values

There can be big opportunity for pricing changes.

Don't think the present owner uses the best plan to price the company's products/services.

Ask yourself this question: Does the company base its prices on how much it thinks what it sells would be worth to itself (to cover costs and make a profit) instead of how much it would be worth to customers?

Carefully examine the competition, and the target customers. Is there room to raise prices, especially if the company improves it pitches to customers about the value it delivers for the prices customers pay? Keep in mind that some customers want to pay more than what a competitor's company charges.

Have you ever shopped for luxury items or professional services? Think about the value from the perspectives of your customers.

Exploit insolvency opportunity.

According to a prolific dealmaker, Arnold S. Goldstein, whose tell-it-like-it-is books and educational materials have guided people for decades: "Approach valuation from the seller's view, an alternative to liquidation. Encourage the seller to enter formal insolvency proceedings, with the buyer acquiring the business at liquidation value. An incentive to the seller could be employment, or a non-compete agreement, or payments out of profits. If you guarantee any debt, limit it consistent with the value of the deal."

Don't forecast revenue to stay the same.

Be prepared for a temporary decline in revenue shortly after you gain control of the business. When a business changes hands, competitors will make a run at your customers and employees. Expect a few customers to take a test drive with your competitors to see if they can get a better deal from them.

Don't expect all the employees to be there for long.

A change in business ownership is sometimes the catalyst for employees to leave for greener pastures. Turnover among the least productive employees is a good thing; you can replace them with people you select, or you might outsource their jobs. Losing good employees, however, is a setback that you should try to avoid.

Immediately upon taking over meet with employees to assure them you want them to stay and that you will listen to their complaints and suggestions.

Don't forecast expenses to remain flat.

Sweetheart deals with suppliers tend to end when a business changes hands. Suppliers that have been reluctant to raise prices or curtail customer service play catch up with the new owner. Immediately identify alternative sources of supply.

Probe for sweetheart deals.

Does the business have a "sweetheart" relationship with any customer, supplier, lender, landlord or employee that gives it an advantage? Don't accept the seller's "No." Investigate.

It's far better to buy a wonderful company at a fair price than a fair company at a wonderful price.

— Warren Buffett

CHAPTER 6

Financing Your Acquisition and the Company

The Pandemic and the recession and its aftermath, including the credit crunch, has resulted in an increase in seller financing, creative financing, asset-based lending, and alternative sources of capital for buyers. This chapter details what is happening and what to do about it. Much more is in my book:

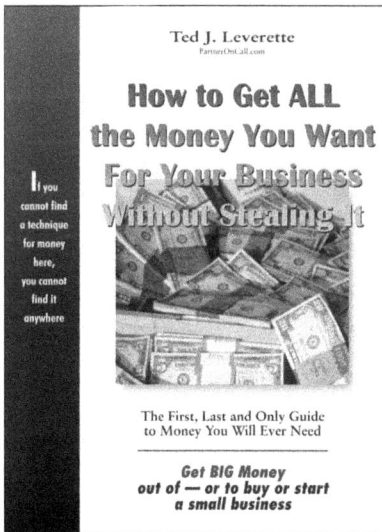

Ted J. Leverette
PartnerOnCall.com

How to Get ALL the Money You Want For Your Business Without Stealing It

If you cannot find a technique for money here, you cannot find it anywhere

The First, Last and Only Guide to Money You Will Ever Need

Get BIG Money out of — or to buy or start a small business

Con artists prey on businesses seeking money.

Beware of con artists posing as loan brokers or venture capitalists.

How to avoid scams:

Most people get taken advantage of because they suspend their common sense for the promise of getting rich quick, or because they do not substantiate what somebody else told them. Naive people believe they can use the courts to save them from paying the price for making a bad decision. The fact is the courts rarely provide relief. Ask your attorney about how much it will cost you to prove with litigation you are right. Then ask him to estimate the probability of you collecting on your judgment, assuming you win. It is bad news. You might pay more than you get! Also ask how much time it will take to collect if you win.

Be wary of these types of investments and promises of capital:

- Those you must buy into immediately or the opportunity will pass

- Opportunities with exceptionally low risk (too good to be true)

- Unreasonable guarantees, especially wild and unsubstantiated claims about potential earnings

- Claims about "proven" concepts

- Up-front fees which do not relate to a specific service you need

- Out-of-state and out-of-country promoters, especially with a P.O. Box address

- Promoters who send you information via Fed X (to avoid mail fraud)

- Businesses with profit history or potential which exceeds 5% of its industry norm

- Incomplete or unclear documentation

- Businesses or individuals who have been bankrupt, have poor credit, or have a history of litigation

- Anybody who will not put everything they say in writing

- Makes assurances about good locations, or the assistance of a professional locator
- References from satisfied customers you cannot substantiate (con artists pay "singers" to pose as happy clients)
- "Guaranteed" loans or equity
- Internet promoters operate outside mail fraud charges and are not easy to track down when they do not deliver on their promises
- Nigerian-letters: Usually unsolicited direct mail to businesses claiming money is available from rich foreigners. The promoters ask you for information about your credit history, including banking and credit card data. Then they fleece you.
- Whenever you hear the words "trust me"
- When a possible partner says, "I have as much to lose as you do"

No complaints at the Better Business Bureau may simply mean none have been filed by people who have been damaged, or the promoter "satisfied" the complainant (which means the BBB removed the bad mark)

If you feel an emotional high because you discover a great deal, you might have met a con artist. If your excitement does not abate quickly after discovering your one-of-a-kind find, you could be in imminent danger of being cheated.

Any good deal should withstand the scrutiny of competent business and legal advisors. Good deals especially require a second opinion. But be careful of relying too much on specialists for a review of the opportunity. Attorneys and accountants can provide wonderful insight and miss the whole point of the review—is the business viable in its entirety, and will it remain so under your management? (Are the risks manageable given your skills?)

The text for this topic is an excerpt from my creative financing book: *How to Get ALL the Money You Want For Your Business Without Stealing It* ™.

Don't buy if the company can't pay for itself.

Why should you purchase a business that can't pay for itself?

Street-smart buyers know that their purchase down payment is the only money they should *have* to invest (except to pay for post-acquisition surprises or to seize exceptional opportunities). It's a costly business-buying mistake if the company's cash flow cannot service its acquisition debt.

Cash flow should service debt, provide reasonable owner salary/ benefits (at prevailing market rates) plus earn a reasonable return *on* your investment.

Don't forever guarantee the entire amount of your note.

Try not to personally guarantee *all* the promissory note, for its entire term, for seller financing.

For the less than street-smart buyer or one lacking a savvy business acquisition advisory team, the company purchaser may have (but did not have to) personally guarantee the entire amount due on the promissory note to seller. A better tactic is to schedule annual decreases in the guarantee of the remaining balance. Keep in mind when deciding how much and for how long you will personally guarantee debt repayment that other personal guarantees may be required, such as trade credit from suppliers, leases, and other sources of financing. Related is the personal collateral that lenders may require borrowers to pledge; be judicious parceling out your guarantees and collateral.

Have a good reason to buy the real estate.

Unless you have a good reason to do so, it is usually not wise to purchase the business' premises at the time you buy the company.

There are two issues involved here. What is the worth of the real estate and who should own it? The seller should obtain an impartial M.A.I. appraisal. In most situations, you should not buy real estate that is the site of the business you purchase. One reason you don't want to own the real estate is that its debt service will eat your cash flow, and the promissory note or mortgage will adversely affect your balance sheet. Moreover, if things go wrong, it's better to be delinquent on rent due to somebody else. Don't tell the seller upfront you don't want the real estate. Later, when you negotiate for the business, show the seller why it is smarter for him to sell the real property to a third-party investor from whom you lease space. This can be a simple item to arrange if you properly communicate it to the seller.

You can purchase a much larger and safer company if you use your money to buy the business, period.

Encourage the seller to find someone else to buy the real estate. If real estate investors are not interested in the property, does it mean they are concerned about the business' capability to pay rent? What does that tell you about the business opportunity?

On the other hand, ignoring for a moment the down payment requirement, some buyers buy the real estate if the mortgage payment is less than the cost to rent the property and/or to accumulate real estate equity while paying down the mortgage. Depending upon the deal, obtaining deal financing can be easier when the real estate is included. Most banks love what they deem good real estate. They can roll the business and the real estate into a 15 to 25-year loan, making the overall payments much less than 10-year financing on the business only.

Milk the company's cash flow.

This applies to business buyers.

Application

To the extent the business you want to acquire can afford it, you can use its cash flow to cover your down payment (since most companies, which are worth buying, generate enough net cash in a couple months) that you promise (in your purchase contract) to hand the seller 60 days after he sells his firm to you.

A variation is to tell the seller that your source of cash (without identifying it as being his business, unless you want to), will come to you in bits and pieces over the next couple of months, so you will commit to making weekly/monthly payments (which you know the seller's business can handle).

Tip

With concurrence from your attorney, you might want to hand the seller, at close of escrow, your post-dated check (which you intend to cover with the business' cash flow).

A variation is to turn over some or all the business' accounts receivable to the seller. This reduces the portion of the down-payment the seller requires from the buyer's funds. The seller collects these accounts receivable.

Warnings

The seller might be too aggressive collecting accounts receivable assigned to him as part of the down payment. This may create ill will with your customers.

Post-dating may not provide you with solid legal footing; the recipient of your check might be able to "prematurely" cash it.

Don't misunderstand cash flow.

Cash flow forecasting is misunderstood by too many people.

Net cash flow is the balance remaining after deducting cash out-flows from cash inflows. Positive is good; negative is not.

Factors influencing net cash flow: Seasonality. Profit vs Negative Cash Flow.

Depreciation pitfall: Insufficient cash or borrowing power to replace assets in the normal course of business.

Profit is not enough to justify the purchase.

It is a big problem, which frequently arises, because forecasters don't realize that company positive net cash flow is insufficient to cover debt service payments when they are due and payable.

Positive cash flow is necessary to meet debt repayment requirements when payments are due. Profit is important but cash flow is more important on a day-to-day basis; negative cash flow can lead to insolvency, which can quickly put the company out of business.

Five C's of raising capital.

Regardless of where you seek funding, your prospective lender or investor will review your creditworthiness.

Application

The basic components of credit analysis, the "Five C's," are listed below. They help you understand what your source of money will evaluate.

Depending on the type of loan and lender or investor, the emphasis will shift among these five components.

1. Capacity (cash flow and collateral) to repay is often the most critical of the five factors; the lender will want to know exactly how you intend to repay the loan; the investor his investment.

2. Capital is the money you personally have invested in your business. It is an indication of how much you have at risk if your business fails.

3. Collateral or guarantees are additional forms of security you can provide the lender; an investor wants to know he will get his money back if your venture fails.

4. Conditions focus on the intended purpose of the loan or equity funding. Will the money be used for working capital, equipment, or inventory? Will it be used for buying out a partner, the company or for physical expansion?

5. Character is the general impression you make on your potential lender and it includes your reputation, experience, education, and the quality of your personal and business references.

Tips

As a condition of making a loan, institutions expect there to be enough excess cash, after covering operating disbursements, to re-pay a loan. Do not be fooled by an accountant's definition of profit as an indicator of cash flow. Profits can be frozen in accounts receivable or in the cost of inventory. Depending on how a business keeps its books, profit can be overstated because sales are booked as income before the cash is received. There is only one way to measure cash flow: Cash-in less cash-out.

Collateral is important, but institutional lenders rarely loan money solely based on it. They expect it to be pledged, but if cash flow cannot be seen to be the sole source of loan payments, no amount of collateral will justify a loan on the best terms. If your loan request emphasizes collateral more than cash flow or other factors as security for the loan, consider applying to an equity (asset) lender.

Institutions will frequently decline a loan request because your loan purpose does not fit their lending guidelines. Lenders prefer to make loans that have proved to be profitable for them.

In addition, institutions tend to be deaf to loan requests aimed at solving a problem you should have anticipated. Plan your cash flow carefully. If you need money to relieve a cash flow crunch, expect your bank to decline your request.

If you ask a bank for money before you need it (to finance growth or inventory, or another reasonable purpose) it is usually available.

Impress your banker with a thorough strategic business plan and financial pro-forma which anticipates capital and managerial talent your business will require for the next stage of its growth.

Asset-based loans.

If you cannot or prefer not to sell an asset to raise cash, use it as collateral for a loan from an asset-based lender. This type of lender makes a loan based on your collateral, instead of your business' cash flow.

Application

The collateral includes, but is not limited to, the following items. The percent of value an asset lender will loan—loan-to-value—appears in parentheses. (These percentages change in accordance with economic conditions.)

- Accounts Receivable (75% to 90% of face value, depending on the creditworthiness of your customers, aging of accounts receivable, and potential delinquency.)

- Inventory (25% to 50% of the cost of raw materials and finished goods if the lender thinks it can readily liquidate the items in the event of a default. 50% to 90% of "retail value" for goods with a strong demand from customers.)

- Notes receivable (50% to 80%, depending upon the quality of the underlying collateral and creditworthiness of the borrower.)

- Equipment and vehicles (60% to 75% of liquidation value.)

- Real property (50% to 85% of quick-sale fair market value; raw land at the lower range; marketable improved property at the higher range.)

Asset-based lenders are more expensive than most other types of lenders. In addition to paying a high rate of interest and points, you might incur costs for an application fee, audit fee, closing costs and asset appraisal.

On the other hand, an asset-based lender may be your *only* source of capital.

Factoring.

This, for business buyers, can be a creative financing technique for acquiring the company but it requires cooperation from sellers (which is not easy to obtain). Once you are in control of the company, however, this financing tactic may be useful to you.

Factoring

Factoring is a technique for raising short-term capital to cover your company's cash requirement.

Application

You sell at a discount, or assign, one or more accounts receivable, with or without recourse, to a factoring company.

The financing agreement between you and the factor stipulates the percentage of the value of the assigned accounts receivable which is available to borrow. The percentage usually ranges from 70% to 85% but can be lower or higher depending on the factor's policies and the creditworthiness of the borrower and the borrower's customers.

You typically pay the factor a steep fee — 3% to 10% per month on the daily balance — until your customers remit payment (to you or the factor, depending upon your agreement with the factor).

Additional fees may apply: an audit fee, closing costs, management fee.

The degree of risk the factor believes it takes by financing your accounts receivable is the basis for the fee you pay. Your credit rating is not as relevant as is the credit rating of your customers.

(If you think about it, retail and other merchants who accept customer payment by credit card "factor" to generate cash. Every time a merchant accepts a credit card, in essence, factoring occurs. The merchant submits to the bank the credit card slips and the bank deposits money into the merchant's account. The bank charges the merchant a fee—usually 3% to 5% of the sale—for collecting from the merchant's customer.)

Advantage

Factors are "expensive" but use of one may mean your company does not need to invest in an internal accounts receivable management department.

Tip

Besides purchasing accounts receivable, handling billing, bookkeeping, and collections, a factor may protect you from losses you would sustain if customers do not pay their bills.

Moreover, some factors loan against your inventory or equipment, even notes receivable you hold.

Shop around. Some factors charge interest plus an "accounts receivable management" fee; others bundle their charge as a percentage of the face amount of the accounts receivable they finance.

Some factors credit part of their fee back to you, depending upon the "quality" and profitability of their relationship with your firm (which includes your customers' paying habits).

Discounting of selected invoices or notes, issued against customers with an established credit history, on a case-by-case basis, is another possibility to discuss with a factor.

Warning

Factoring, because of its expense, is a short-term solution to your financial crisis.

Unless the product you sell earns an exceptionally high profit margin, the interest and the fees you pay the factor can quickly erode the financial stability of your company.

Think of using a factor like using an antibiotic; over-use can make you more susceptible to the problem you want to eradicate.

Customer provides equity.

This, for business buyers, can be a creative financing technique for acquiring the company but it requires pre-acquisition cooperation from sellers if you need to raise more capital for your investment from one or more of the company's employees. Once you are in control of the company, this financing tactic may be useful to you anytime during your ownership.

Customer financing means one or more of your business' customers invest in your company.

Application

Your customers must think your firm offers them one or more unique advantage which they, the customers, cannot easily replicate by patronizing your company's competitors.

Or customers must believe they can make a profitable investment by becoming a co-investor in the business.

Advantages

Customer investment enables you to cash out some of your ownership of your business—to personally use the money, or to employ it to grow your company.

Your company gets cash, additional management skills and favorable pricing.

The customer/investor gets diversification, an insight into your business and a nice return on investment.

Strengthens customer commitment to your firm.

Tip

You will need a cash-rich customer, or one with access to capital, for this to work.

As an inducement to get customer funding, offer the customer special terms when the customer purchases products or services from your firm. These include:

- Price protection

- Priority order fulfillment

- Extended warranty

- Better return or allowance provision

- Private label merchandise (your products bear their name)

Another inducement that may attract capital from customers is to offer a strategic alliance between their company and your firm. A strategic alliance improves each participant's business by *diversifying* each firm's products, talent, locations, marketing, production, etc.

Warning

When offering incentives to customers to provide funds, resist lengthening credit terms or discounting the price your customers pay for products and services; this erodes the financial security of your business and their investment.

Collateral probably means more than you think it does.

Lenders (and some investors) seek protection from loss of their money by getting you to pledge collateral to secure your payment to them according to the terms of your agreement.

Application

Collateral comes in many forms. You probably have more than you recognize.

To name a few you can pledge, using a lien or an assignment to protect your source of funds:

- Accounts receivable
- Bills of lading
- Chattel mortgage
- Commission
- Equipment, machinery, vehicles, etc.
- Factor's liens
- Franchise agreement
- Insurance cash value
- Insurance settlement
- Intellectual property (copyright, trademark, patent, trade secret)
- Inventory

- Lease (equipment, vehicles, real property)
- License agreement
- Marketable securities
- Personal assets (i.e., jewelry, art, antiques, and other collectibles)
- Note receivable
- Real property
- Rent
- Royalty
- Tax refund
- The business' name, website, telephone number, and lease to its premises
- Trust deed or mortgage
- Trust receipt
- Warehouse receipt
- Collateral pledged by a third party

Don't underestimate the deal killing power of financing.

50% of buy/sell transactions, where there was a seller and buyer who reached agreement on everything except acquisition financing, failed to close due to lack of financing. Financing (and lack of it) is the number one reason why businesses fail. Of course, the underlying reasons may relate to poor management or insufficient demand for the company's product, among others. But even well managed firms with strong customer demand fail because of improperly structured financing.

100% seller financing is unlikely and probably unwise.

A wise business buyer won't buy a business unless the seller finances part of the purchase. How much the seller finances will be subject to the availability of outside financing (this relates to the business' ability to pay) and to negotiation between the buyer/seller.

Don't assume seller financing is a good thing.

If a bank or other source of financing won't fund your acquisition, maybe you are going to make a buying mistake. It's a good idea to investigate alternative sources of financing even if the seller volunteers to finance your deal. What you learn will sharpen your due diligence and dealmaking. A nice byproduct of this is you might discover sources of financing your business can use after you buy it.

Don't get too excited about an SBA loan.

SBA financing has enabled many people who otherwise could not have gotten into business to own a business. Most of them were successful.

On the other hand, loan loss rates (depending upon the comparison period) are several times, to as much as eight times, worse than for commercial banks.

Which means the SBA helps a lot of people do dumb deals.

The SBA makes loans that risk-averse, profit-seeking lenders decline.

Have a good understanding about your business' capability to generate sufficient cash flow to retire debt and to provide a return on and of your investment.

Do your homework for SBA-guaranteed financing.

The best place to begin (or go right now if you're thinking about the SBA while dealmaking) is the Small Business Administration website. Don't rely on Google or any other resource until you've learned at the SBA website; there simply is too much erroneous information touted by people and organizations who want you to think they know what you need to know.

For example, a business valuation company answered a prospective client's question: "Is it true the bank has to choose the appraisal firm if someone is getting an SBA guarantee loan?" Here is the appraiser's response: The bank must approve but not necessarily select. The borrower can propose the appraiser and pay the fee, so he has some major influence on the decision. Since we do not know each other and are completely independent with no prior relationship, the bank *may* accept the recommendation of the borrower.

The keyword in the appraiser's response is "may."

And here are other points of view:

An *SBA Product Specialist* at a national bank says: "He's not entirely wrong . . . but why risk it? There is a cost to review it and if for any reason we don't want it, we require another appraisal. Sounds like a waist of $$."

A loan officer at another SBA-approved national bank says: "Unless it's ordered by the bank, it will not be able to be used for financing purposes. It's fine if he wants to order his own appraisal, but he will end up having to pay for a 2nd one once he approaches the bank for financing."

The bank must choose the appraisal firm if you are getting an SBA loan. Be cautious of people demanding fees during the application process.

Author and dealmaker, **John Martinka**, *Martinka Consulting*, advises: "The banks handle it."

Okay, do you see what I mean about doing your homework?

The **Lewis Kappes: SBA Digest**, published by a law firm, is one of the most useful resources for me. Google it. Read the blog. Subscribe to the e-newsletter.

At the time this book is being written the SBA website offers its **Lender Match** (formerly LINC), which is a free online referral tool that connects small businesses with participating SBA-approved lenders.

Use creative financing.

Employ creative financing to limit your risk and to increase your return on investment.

Here's an example of creative financing for the purchase/sale of a distribution firm. It was put together by Terry Cuff, a business broker in Bellevue, WA. This deal is a tax-free exchange—privately-held stock for publicly traded stock. The seller, a privately held company, distributes drugs. It has a well-established customer base. It earned $1 million adjusted cash flow and was absentee run. The deal structure:

- $4,600,000 Price

- $4,100,000 Value of publicly traded shares seller received from buyer

- $ 250,000 Purchaser's assumption of the liabilities of seller's business

- $ 250,000 Purchaser's funds at closing provided to seller

The purchaser provided the seller common shares in the purchaser's firm. The shares had a history of increasing in value (earnings per share) at or above 20% per year. The seller's firm was merged into the purchaser's company 60 days after the sale. The SEC restricts for one year the sale of the securities which the seller received. To generate tax-free cash, the seller pledged his publicly traded shares to a bank. The bank loaned him $2,000,000 on the restricted securities without additional collateral (i.e., personal guarantee). The term of the loan was 2 years at prime rate. This transaction provided the seller a good return on his investment because the value of the public company's shares increased at a rate greater than the seller earned from the company he sold. Because the transaction was structured as a tax-free exchange, the seller (recipient of the publicly traded shares) deferred capital gains tax until he sold the securities.

Don't accept the bank's proposal without shopping.

Shop around with several sources of financing. Compare the terms of their offering. Negotiate reasonable changes (e.g., "Lender X offers such and such; can you?").

Don't feel guilty for being disappointed in banks.

An *Inc. Magazine* poll revealed: About 2/3 of businesses are not satisfied with their banking relationship and 3/4 of these businesses think their bad banking relationship is a threat to their business and an impediment to growth. Many businesses are turning away from banks. "We are being more creative in finding money elsewhere in retaliation for being jerked around at our bank." The smaller the company, the more likely you are to turn to those sources.

Mark Twain defined a banker as "a friend who lends you an umbrella and asks for it back when it looks like it's going to rain."

Verify that financing will occur.

What's the likelihood of the expiration or change of financing, especially if it is dictated by the source of financing?

Sometimes what seemed to be a worthwhile acquisition sours if the buyer did not, before and after buying, adequately evaluate and structure the company's financing. Lenders, especially banks and private sources of financing, take advantage of too many borrowers. Therefore, we recommend that buyers, before buying, estimate the cash reserve or borrowing power they will need in the event of a cash crunch.

Default triggers can shoot down you and your company.

Default triggers are events that cause your lender (such as a bank) to call your loan or refuse to grant additional credit, even though more credit is available to you. Default triggers relate to promises (covenants) you make to the lender in your financing documents.

Financial Covenants

Your lender wants early warning of your potential problems, so it may require you to maintain and report specific ratios for:

- Current assets to current liabilities

- Debt to net worth

- Cash flow

- Interest coverage (profit before tax and interest expense)

Your lender may require you not to exceed limits for:

- Total debt

- Capital expenditures

- Management compensation

In setting financial covenants, lenders rely on their financing experience. They refer to your industry's performance ratios to evaluate your firm.

Default Triggers

Usual indicators of current or pending trouble include:

- Failure to pay principal, interest, or fees when due

- Insolvency or bankruptcy

- Subsequent imposition of a lien on your assets

- Failure to pay taxes when due

- Breach of a provision of your financing agreement

- Death of yourself or a co-signer of the financing agreement

- Termination of employees who the lender deems essential to the success of your firm

- Occurrence of something that increases your ERISA liability

- Occurrence of something that exposes you to liability in relation to EPA (i.e., toxic waste, hazardous materials, etc.)

Tips

Be certain your lender makes loans to businesses in your industry. A lender offsets its lack of knowledge of an industry by charging more for a loan and forcing onerous covenants upon borrowers.

Ask your potential lender early in the application process if it intends to sell your loan on the secondary market. If so, your lender will not have much leeway to negotiate onerous covenants.

Before you sign the loan paperwork and then run out to spend the money, compare your business' historical performance and policies to the loan covenants—as if you borrowed the money a few years ago. If your firm would not have satisfied the covenants then, will it later?

Sometimes not getting a loan is better for your survival.

Don't be squeezed by a line of credit.

Bank lines of credit problems are common.

Beware of companies that are too dependent on a bank line of credit (or factoring). Is it too expensive? Do the financing terms hamper the business? Even the best banks sometimes reduce or cancel credit lines for well-run, profitable companies. And while you're thinking about borrowing, wonder why a particular line of credit is necessary. What does it say about the management of the business' cash flow?

There are blacklists.

Banks may blacklist individual companies and entire industries.

Banks and other sources of financing rarely own up to it but nearly all of them intentionally decline loan applications because of the characteristics of the applicant or the kind and location of the business. Your professional advisors might have insight, which, if you didn't get before buying, it is wise to get afterwards.

Don't sell your assets.

If you don't have enough cash for the down payment, before you sell an asset to raise cash, ask the seller if he will make a trade. It may be easier, quicker and have tax advantages.

Don't ignore the effect of principal payments.

Buyers risk a cash flow crisis if they fail to realize that *principal* payments are not a tax-deductible expense; they consume cash. That's why it is important to compute after-tax profit—to see how much company cash *will* be (if you do this before buying) or *is* (if you bought the company) available to make principal payments on acquisition and other debt.

Have a good reason (and a piggy bank) if you agree to pay more than 50% of after-tax profit to service acquisition debt.

Don't borrow too much.

There are numerous rules that professional business buyers keep in mind. How much debt can you and/or your business acquisition afford? As much as you and the business' cash flow can handle may not be prudent. Do not agree to pay more than 50% of the business' after-tax profit to service acquisition debt.

Don't get caught short.

Anticipate, if you want to avoid inadequate cash or borrowing power, for asset replacement.

This risky situation occurs if the forecasts you made, and the inquiries you made with sources of financing, before buying turn out, after buying, to be wrong.

Find and validate potential for growth.

Karl Tettmann, author, and architect of the *GROWTH*™ *Technique*, advises:

Think about validating potential growth before you buy and for sure post-acquisition.

As the buyer who is evaluating a business, you will spot businesses that are stuck in their own ruts; we call it "stuck in the trenches," meaning they are doing the busy work . . . daily tasks, putting out fires and doing what needs to be done. The hours fly by turning days into weeks and then months. The business may have, for a few years, shown slow growth or it may be hovering around the same revenues. This is a clue that the business might have more potential for growth.

As a buyer, a key to unlocking growth is to analyze the potential for growth. A company that has not been growing as much as the buyer wishes may not be the fault of the business or its management; they may have run out of ambition, energy or been at it too long. And that's where the opportunity lies. In projecting reasonable achievable growth, look forward three years. That is usually the optimum measure, because by then your company has had enough time to surpass the break-even point for new growth and showing good returns. By year five you have alternatives: You could sell the company for more than you paid for it because you have increased its value and its investment opportunity. Or, because your company is ready for the next growth phase, you can take it to the next level.

Preparing for super-growth is where you lean on your advisors to do the research and to validate that there is a reasonable rate of growth evidenced by cash flow projections and break-even analyses. Company managers too often overlook this kind of planning because they lack knowledge regarding the benefits of delegating the market assessment to an independent professional advisor. It's a skillful process that begins with assessing the company's existing data and then designing new strategic and marketing initiatives to grow. Evaluating a business' potential growth determines the effort, cost, investment, and time necessary to achieve the target growth and, most importantly, relates new growth to the additional cash investment necessary to profitably grow.

Here's where the gem lies. By validating the growth of a company, the buyer can forecast whether the business has more potential than the seller might see or want to pursue; hence the business could be worth more to the buyer than the seller thinks it is worth.

Don't try for excessive growth.

Does the company's sales growth exceed its industry average? Faster growing businesses risk failure if there is not enough money, borrowing power or talent to handle it. Some of the risks include cash flow crunches, overwhelmed employees and suppliers, shortages of resources, operating procedures tripping over one another, customer dissatisfaction if service falters.

Use it but don't tell sellers about the 50% rule.

Don't tell sellers about our 50% rule: "Buyers should not pay more than 50% of after-tax profit to service acquisition debt." If, upfront, you reveal this street-smart business buying rule to sellers or brokers, most sellers and brokers will stop talking to you. Spring the 50% rule on the seller later, after you and the seller have invested a considerable amount of time in due diligence. The best time to introduce the 50% rule to the seller is when you both have agreed on the purchase price (typically after the seller sees the *Price Fairness Opinion* that you obtained). At this stage, buyer and seller are structuring the terms of purchase.

Don't give your unconditional personal guarantee.

Resist giving an *unconditional* personal guarantee on seller financing of the purchase or on anything else (e.g., lease, supplier contracts). Sometimes you cannot avoid pledging personal assets or income as collateral. It is a risk/reward proposition. If the benefits of the deal overcome the risks (especially possible versus certain risks), you might be foolish to abort the deal.

Monthly debt service payments may not be advisable.

If the business is cyclical or seasonal, schedule the amount and timing of payments on acquisition debt to coincide with the business' positive cash flow.

Don't use personal funds to pay acquisition debt.

If the business' cash flow cannot handle all the payments to retire acquisition debt, find another business to buy that can pay for itself.

Don't make unlikely forecasts.

The budgets and/or forecasts are inconsistent or improbable too often for too many companies.

People write an invitation to a business acquisition disaster when there is too big a variance between their pre- and post- acquisition budgeting and forecasting, and when wishful thinking or incompetent analysis is the basis for their budgets and forecasts.

BTW, according to *accountingtools.com*, "the key difference between a budget and a forecast is that the budget is a plan for where a business wants to go, while a forecast is the indication of where it is actually going."

Proceed using these analyses and forecasts.

Break-even point analysis and cash flow forecasting is necessary.

Break-even calculations can be the first step in analysis and planning. It's a tool to make an initial judgment about whether a plan is within the realm of feasibility, and the degree to which changes will affect profit.

When business buyers and company owners realize how this simple, yet rarely used, formula enables them to make better decisions, they try it. Once they experience its power, they become addicted to it.

With *Break-even Point and Cash Flow Analysis* an owner can easily and accurately:

- Obtain a desired profit

- Plan cost reductions

- Examine expansion feasibility

- Determine profit margins

- Know how much cost can be incurred at no risk

- Establish a selling price

- Manage labor costs

- Decide on credit terms granted to customers

A well-designed *cost* accounting system is helpful; typical *general* accounting systems do not provide sufficient detail re interrelated activities and do not associate revenue and costs to the company's products and services.

Break-even is the point or level of financial activity at which expenditure equals income or the value of an investment equals its cost, with the result that there is neither a profit nor a loss.

Don't be financially shortsighted.

In business, you either use your money or other people's money (OPM). Buyers lose their opportunity to buy because they do not have sufficient capital to purchase and operate the company, or they do not know how to use creative financing.

Your lack of capital for the business you own or want to own is a hindrance you can overcome with street-smart knowledge of finance. Study our creative financing book, so you don't have to use as much of your money or personal borrowing power to buy and operate the business:

How to Get ALL the Money You Want For Your Business Without Stealing It ™

CHAPTER 7

Negotiating and Dealmaking

How you design and handle negotiating and dealmaking determines your success.

This chapter details what is happening and what to do about it.

The playing field is tilted against buyers.

You cannot achieve the best deal possible if you play on an unlevel field.

Level the Playing Field

Buyer	**Buyer Competition**	**Seller**
Experience		Knows the Business
Capabilities		Prepared Himself
Money		Many Buyers
Advisory Team		Advisory Team

VALUE

Business

ADVANTAGES

Not shown in the image above is the contribution business brokers add to the sellers' advantages. You will read about this throughout this book.

Do not misconstrue what you read in this book. It *is* advisable for buyers, while searching for companies for sale, to stay in touch with brokers and other seller-intermediaries; doing so keeps buyers connected to sellers that might not appear while buyers are looking for businesses for sale by-owner on the hidden market.

Okay, so on with the story: You are a buyer. Out there are sellers. You want to buy a business. You have a problem. It's buyer competition.

Savvy buyers effectively access the hidden market because they want to avoid most, if not all, buyer competition. The hidden market is where to identify potential sellers, so the buyer can be first on scene. It is also where to find unadvertised businesses for sale by-owner. The hidden market can put you in touch with, depending upon the industry, up to 80% of the *profitable* companies that are sold (the keyword being "sold" versus for sale).

Start thinking in terms of US and THEM. Most observers say the playing field is tilted in the seller's favor. Buyers have an uphill climb.

Here's why sellers start with advantages:

- They know more about their company and industry than you, and few will tell you everything;

- They have prepared themselves and their company for sale;

- They think there are a lot of buyers for it (which is often true);

- They have an advisory team. And maybe a business broker represents them.

You have to know what you bring to the table, and effectively present it to sellers and their representatives:

- Experience

- Capabilities

- Money

- Acquisition advisory team.

This is your value. When the seller and the seller's team perceive your value as being worth the seller's business, a deal can take place and the business can change hands.

Phases and obstacles through which you must navigate.

The business broker's primary allegiance is to business sellers.

A *Business Buyer Advocate* (that's me) levels the playing field for buyers using my proprietary *Street-Smart 22-Step Acquisition Sequence* ™.

It helps you navigate through:

1. Searching—so you meet more companies than you can find on your own.

2. Due diligence—evaluating the owner, the company and the transaction.

3. Financing—exploring creative financing & assessing sources of financing.

4. Pricing businesses for sale—pricing differs from valuation.

5. Dealmaking—doing what it takes to achieve a profitable done deal.

6. Post-acquisition due diligence and transition management.

The big picture.

"Buyers" are not buyers until they achieve a done deal. Until then they are searchers.

Labeling them "searchers" can keep our eyes and minds on reality. But "searching" is not enough.

Finding is what it takes for the possibility of done deals. When you find them, you must negotiate for them.

We begin with negotiations because if you don't get this right, right from the first moment, you might not buy the right business the right way. You'll probably either buy the wrong business or buy the right business the wrong way.

Our focus is on small and midsize businesses.

Negotiation is how people resolve their differences.

Stages of negotiation.

This overview, from SkillsYouNeed.com, puts it into perspective:

To achieve a desirable outcome, it may be useful to follow a structured approach to negotiation. For example, in a work situation a meeting may need to be arranged in which all parties involved can come together.

1. The process of negotiation includes the following stages:

2. Preparation

3. Discussion

4. Clarification of goals

5. Negotiate towards a Win-Win outcome

6. Agreement

7. Implementation of a course of action

It's a good idea to use the link above to see the explanations.

Let's consider how savvy buyers negotiate with sellers.

You're in control.

Or *they* are.

Searching for businesses to buy can be frustrating. But it doesn't have to be . . . if searchers deploy best practices to handle the initial communications and interactions between searchers, advisors, brokers, sellers, and business owners.

Let's begin with performance anxiety. Not *that* one. This one:

- Everybody is nervous about negotiating.

- Fear of failure; being taken advantage of; looking foolish or naïve; self-defeating behavior.

That's why I suggest asking questions. Instead of assertions or proposals. Polite and appropriate questions instantly move the stress to the other side of the dealmaking table.

Timely silences and pauses slow and calm the pace. And can people to negotiate against themselves. That includes you! Talking too much can cost you. Big time. (Being quiet is a tactic to think about. A lot.)

Illegitimate searchers.

Beware of the seminars and coaches pitching "secrets" and schemes to the gullible, such as "get-rich-quick-with-no-risk" and "buy-a-business-using-none-of-your-money."

The conning tactics take place online, especially with clickbait on LinkedIn and Facebook. YouTube is nirvana for conmen.

Count among the fakers the poseurs spawning (or reappearing since the last financial crisis) touting their "expertise" at buying or financing SMBs. And if you join / hire / pay them, you, too, can achieve miracles. Do it today, to be one of the few select people they will help. You can get their dealmaking secrets at a discount . . . if you pay them now. Limited time offer!!!

Instead, invest a few hundred dollars in the most realistic how-to books for searchers and buyers. You'll see the "secrets" in the context of reality.

I suppose I should be flattered that most of the get-rich-quick and buy-businesses-with-no-money pitchmen have read and then adapted, to their purposes, some of the content within my how-to books.

I like it when truly professional and moral professionals in our service sector use my materials, but I don't respect the poseurs who take advantage of unsuspecting people. Especially when people are scared and trying to protect their financial security.

Expect transparency. Ask for it. Evaluate it. Run, don't walk, away when you don't get it.

There's a big difference between knowing something and knowing what to do about it.

Get actionable, affordable and legitimate guidance.

Searching like an amateur.

Proclaiming "I'm agnostic" probably won't be a fast pass into heaven. And it could be a slow, circuitous way for the "I'm agnostic" searchers proclaiming they want to buy any kind of business under the sun, sea and outer space. Not taking a stand is a good way to go nowhere fast.

- "I'll know it when I see it."

- "Show me everything!"

- "Let me go to school on your dime."

In my dealmaking world, collaborating with serious searchers, people who buy mature, profitable and fairly-priced businesses, "I'm agnostic" is a sure sign of an amateur. Usually the hopeful searchers graduating from the get-rich-with-no-money seminars/books/mentors/coaches/etc.

Ask brokers what they think about this.

Desirability.

"Desirability" is hugely important to people wanting to sell or buy a SMB. Here are a few factors affecting desirability:

- No status, rough or dirty work

- Respectable and satisfactory

- Challenging & attractive workplace

- The company needs specific (technical) talent to operate

- The company creates an image of sleaze, which some people find disgusting (porn & telemarketing, etc.)

- To be attractive it has to make a lot of money as there is no "sex appeal" to it

- It's a company that people look up to and it only requires general business skill to operate

- Business that deals with unattractive products or services (waste treatment businesses as an example)

- Company perceived as solid but run of the mill

- Highly profitable company in great location that allows spouse to brag about what business their spouse is in

- Sexy, flashy, fashionable business which "everybody" wants to buy

- Company has to be marketed to attract buyer, but is steady performer in a healthy industry

- Company has good profile in business community, excellent C.E.L.B.S relationships, regularly attracts unsolicited offers to buy.

Why some buyers seek troubled businesses.

According to USBX, Inc., there are seven reasons why buyers may seriously consider purchasing your troubled business:

The buyer may already have an existing business like yours and, by combining the two, be able to operate at lower cost.

The buyer may seek to acquire any number of your operating assets, such as desirable customer bases, complementary product lines, proprietary technology, key locations, staff, name, URL, or other tangible or intangible assets.

The buyer may have expertise in restructuring or repositioning businesses, and has a plan to make your business profitable either by streamlining operations or through integration with their existing companies.

The buyer may decide that it is more feasible to acquire your business, to invest in it and make it successful, than it would be to build a comparable business from the ground up.

The buyer may have sufficient finance sources to carry the loss until your business becomes profitable.

The buyer may have lower financial expectations and feel that, with minor cutbacks and a small investment, modest profits are achievable.

The buyer may be looking for a loss to offset taxation obligations.

Age discrimination.

It's is a reality for employees and job searchers. But not for people buying and owning small and midsize businesses. Gray hair is a plus because it connotes experience. And people over 50 have something, arguably, more valuable: Motivation and commitment. Commitment to success, because their alternative is bleak: Losing their money and unable to get a worthwhile job. They simply can't afford to fail.

Don't ask dumb questions.

If you want to improve your results with sellers and brokers, emulate the savviest searchers. See my other book for facts, tips and strategies (and lots of don'ts): *How to Prepare Yourself and Find the Right Business to Buy*.

"What's your biggest weakness?" the wantrepreneur asks the seller of a SMB.

Seller: "Interviewing potential buyers."

Wantrepreneur: "And besides that?"

Seller: "Follow up questions."

Questions to uncover the truth and get what you want.

These are the BIG-PICTURE questions; they tap into emotions. Which puts into perspective EVERYTHING else. Get these right and good things happen.

These questions precede and go beyond the typical due diligence questions, which are fact-focused more than emotional (unless you unwisely make them emotional).

These kinds of questions are useful for negotiating.

Don't ask yes/no questions. Ask open-ended questions.

Some of these questions are similar. It's because their alternate phrasings make sense in some situations.

- You don't have to ask all of them; but knowing them will alert you to detect the answers without asking.

Ask Yourself

Negotiations begin by asking yourself. Your answers can establish your position; your wants; your go/no-go limits.

What's it worth to *you*? (The company and the opportunity.)

How much can you afford to lose?

What is your monthly lost-opportunity cost (the income you forego while searching)?

What about buyer competition?

Why waste time with brokers and sellers who are not forthcoming with the kinds of info buyers need?

Can you afford to lose the deal?

Have you assembled a competent advisory team?

How will you nourish your relationship with brokers and sellers?

When is the most opportune time to hire tax and legal counsel?

Why ARE you looking for an acquisition?

Do you have the proven capability to successfully manage the kind of company you want to own?

Do you have the money and borrowing power to buy and fund the company?

What are you doing to be a better negotiator?

What can cause a fatal case of buyer fever?

But what about when brokers and sellers answer your questions with questions?

What emotion determines whether buyers or sellers win more? (Motivation) How do you test for motivation?

Could you, tomorrow, sell the company you bought yesterday . . . on terms equal to or better than the deal you made?

Who cares what somebody claims to be the value of a company if nobody wants to own it?

What do you do when brokers don't represent what you want to buy?

Do you have an unblinking eye over the entire playing field? Can you see and anticipate what's coming?

Not enough evidence? Ask for it.

What should searchers disclose, how and when?

Why do you think brokers, owners and sellers read my how-to books written for buyers?

Have you read my books? Why not? If so, do you think it is a good idea to talk to me about deploying the tactics . . . before you interact with brokers and sellers?

Ask Sellers

Why did you get into this kind of business? What kept you at? Why change now?

How did your company do during the recession? What about your surviving competitors?

What kinds of marketing did you try that didn't pay off?

What's going on / coming up in your community and in your industry that is going to be good or not so good over the next couple of years?

If you were to keep your company instead of selling it now, what would you do that you believe would make it more profitable and valuable between now and whenever it's time for you to exit?

How do you feel about what we've been discussing, where we might go next?

Would you please elaborate on that?

I'm not sure if I understand what you're trying to accomplish?

What do you think would be the findings if you did an employee satisfaction survey?

After you provide me with the information, I need to begin due diligence, how long will it take you to assemble or arrange other things I might need, such as seeing your list of customers, employees, and suppliers? What about interviewing them?

What do you want me to do?

Why is it so important for you to get that?

Looking back, what would you have done differently that might have made your company even stronger than it is today?

If you were me, how would you see what I'm offering you for what you're offering me?

Is there another way we can handle this for a win-win deal?

How can we make this work for us?

Why is that so important to you? Is it a deal killer?

What will you do if we cannot reach an agreement?

What can we do to make a win-win deal?

What alternatives can we consider?

What do I need to know to see . . . like you do . . . the value of your company?

What do you think will be the best way for you to help me transition into your company?

Where's the fat that could be trimmed without unmanageable adverse effect?

Do you think your company, and you and I, could do better if I am initially an investor/working partner? Or is now the best time for you to exit?

It's been a good first meeting, exchanging information about each other and your company. How much time to do you need to gather the basic documents I need to see? (Tax returns, financial statements, premises lease, restrictive agreements, etc.)

How have you handled employees who weren't performing well enough? What about employees who couldn't or wouldn't improve enough? What about troublesome employees?

What's the best way your company targets and then sells to customers?

What, exactly, do you think causes new customers to discover you and then do business with you? How about retention: why don't they shop elsewhere?

How much time can you give me for due diligence? Can you commit to me that you will promptly provide the information I need so we can get through due diligence within your time frame? What have you done to assemble the kinds of information buyers need to evaluate?

Is there anyone else but you who has or will have a say in the deal we want to make?

What have you done to determine whether your landlord will approve the assignment of your lease? How will the terms of the lease differ? How has the landlord treated you over the years? What is the financial stability of the landlord?

Why is your company for sale?

Why are we talking about the possibility of me investing or buying your business?

What have you done / do you do to track the performance of your marketing and sales?

What's been the evolution of the needs of the kinds of customers you serve? How about suppliers?

What about employee productivity?

To what degree is the revenue cyclical or seasonal? What's the biggest risk to consistent revenue?

How involved have you been in the trade associations serving your industry? To what degree do you have friendly relationships with your competitors?

How do you see the competitive advantages your company has over the competition? What about sustainability? How have competitors responded re _____? What would your top competitor say is your competitive advantage . . . and for his company?

What about a customer survey? Suppliers? Landlord?

What happens in your company when you are not available, such as sick or on vacation?

What kinds of liabilities are there that are not shown on the financial statements? Things like accrued PTO.

How do you think your employees will react when they find out your company is for sale? What about after its sale? What about customers and suppliers? What about your strongest competitors?

What kind of indemnity are you going to provide me in case something bad arises after closing that you didn't warn me about? Or that you couldn't have known, such losing key employees, customers, or suppliers?

Is there anything related to me, or my training or experiences that you think is *not* good enough to successfully manage your company?

What would you do if you were me?

To what degree is your company dependent upon you for day-to-day operation?

How about dependency re employees, customers, suppliers, location?

Could you help me understand why you don't want me to interview _____? What if I can suggest ways to do it that won't let people know I want to buy your business? Can you see why it's important to me that I know what I'm going to get?

To what degree has your company documented the procedures in use for employees, etcetera? What needs to be done for more efficiency?

Considering what I'm offering (price, terms, concessions, security, timing), is there any reason why it isn't a good way to go for you and me?

What do you think your advisor will say about my offer (or whatever)?

I like your company but I'm having trouble with the _____. Can you help me see what you're offering is reasonable and fair for me?

Can you help me understand what concerns you?

Could you help me understand the methodology you used to arrive at your asking price?

What's included in the price? (Assets, transition, consulting, etc.)

How much seller financing makes sense for you?

What's your rationale (your reason) for that?

How about some supporting evidence?

What else do you think I should know about _____?

What can we do to keep the ball moving toward a win-win deal?

How do the terms of the deal we're arguing about compare to other buy/sell transactions?

Would such and such price be acceptable to you? Why not?

I'm not sure if I understand what you're trying to accomplish?

Can we consider why your proposal does not provide me with enough return on investment?

Who should own or lease the real property/real estate?

How, specifically, do your company's competitive advantages pay off for you in the marketplace?

What are the issues, the obstacles to our agreement?

How do our respective priorities differ?

What ways we can exchange benefits?

What will YOU do if I do not invest in or buy your business?

Is there any information that you have not disclosed to me that might have an adverse bearing on the viability or the value of the business for sale?

I'm going to repeat myself: Ask **everyone** you interview . . . and then again ask sellers before your legal counsel begins drafting purchase documents:

Is there any information that you have not disclosed to me that might have an adverse bearing on the viability or the value of the business for sale?

Money isn't the driver.

Having for decades surveyed owners, sellers, searchers and business buyers I can tell you that money is not at the top of the reasons why they, respectively, want to sell their company or buy and operate their own business. Shrewd buyers carefully evaluate the sellers' situations and then appeal to their non-financial needs. This is not to suggest buyers should not pay fair market value. But don't let buyer fever raise your offer beyond what's reasonable. Makes sense, doesn't it?

Motivation rules!

Whomever is most motivated to make the deal is most likely to acquiesce to the other side of the dealmaking table. Therefore, my clients search and find owners who are HIGHLY motivated to sell. We don't take advantage. Everyone gets enough of what they want.

How do we test for motivation? We begin by asking people tell us what they want. And then we ask why they want it. In both cases we encourage them to elaborate; to be more specific. And then we discreetly continue to test for motivation . . . all the way to the day we order legal counsel to prepare the purchase documents.

How to avoid being taken.

Nourish win-win relationships when the going gets bumpy. Spoiler Alert: Expect a few surprises that you will like.

Relationships rule!

Begin early, and continually digress from business-talk . . . schmoozing about your personal life . . . family, fun, pets, adventure . . . how something you see in the seller's office reminds you of a personal story . . . anything except money and business.

Revealing your personal life can build trust, especially if the seller reciprocates.

Reciprocity.

It's a good idea to realize that what you dish out can come back to you in kind. Fairness encourages fairness.

Sellers who don't share are likely to hide the ball . . . about their company, its history and future . . . and your risk.

What's the seller's problem?

I'm serious. What's the owner trying to accomplish? Think about it. The problem is their business; they don't want it anymore. Help owners solve that problem and you'll own their company, and they'll get what they want. And while you're thinking about it, focus less on the business; focus on the emotional state in which owners and sellers find themselves.

Detect how time will affect the other side. One of the most important facts you must detect is how time will affect the other side of your dealmaking table.

Savvy company owners and their brokers create a **seller's** market by attracting multiple buyers who must compete with one another. Sometimes the dumbest buyer wins the bidding war. (Of course, this is wonderful if you're a seller.)

So, what's a buyer to do? Look for competition posed by sellers of other companies. It doesn't have to be the same kind of company with which you're negotiating. When the time is right, discreetly and tactfully let the other side of your dealmaking table know they aren't the only game in town.

Another way to beat buyer competition is to be the seller's first choice among the field of buyers. You do that by properly handling yourself with the seller and the seller's representatives. Don't be obnoxious. Collaboration is better than head-butting.

But how to put into practice "collaboration?" How about "interest-based negotiation?" Attorney Janice Green says: Interest-based negotiation is a way of identifying your "big picture" desires and coming up with alternative routes to meet them. It's having people negotiate from their interests rather than from positions.

Business buyers and sellers should make a list of their respective interests. Next, Janice Green says: "Next you exchange those lists at a joint session and each side has an opportunity to ask questions about the other's interests."

Note the keyword: ASK.

And, she suggests, that someone (other than the negotiators) observe and try to encourage agreements.

Say to the seller: What if I do such-and-such? How can you reciprocate? Or this: What can we do to make a win-win deal?

When it's clear to everyone that negotiating is at play.

Buyers and sellers make big mistakes while negotiating because of their inaccurate assumptions about the other side of the dealmaking table. Therefore, the due diligence and negotiating tactics my clients use is question-based. Ask, don't guess.

Negotiation is the **glue** that holds everything else together.

Communication is how negotiators **apply** it to people.

Here are a few observations and tips that are so important I want to emphasize them now:

- Business buyers have more at risk and more to lose than sellers.

- Most deals fall through, sometimes at the 11th hour. That's why searchers should continue searching until the closing/completion of their deal.

- Don't negotiate with yourself. Don't suggest alternatives unless it's necessary to keep the deal moving. Your signal to propose alternatives is when the seller refuses your proposal but . . . before you suggest an alternative . . . ask the seller to suggest alternatives.

- Focusing too much on what's in it for me is among the biggest mistakes made by buyers and sellers.

Here's a question to ask everyone you interview . . . and then **again** ask **sellers** before your legal counsel begins drafting purchase documents:

"Is there any information that you have not disclosed to me that might have an adverse bearing on the viability or the value of the business for sale?"

Too many business buyers don't pose that question to everyone. Everyone.

Worse, too many buyers let people get away with a non-definitive answer.

Buyers correctly asking that question at the right time will see a road map for further inquiry. Not asking that question (and then verifying the response) is why so many dumb deals occur.

What's a worthwhile done deal?

Have you thought about . . . what's the **proof** that you negotiated a **good-enough** deal? Well, **could** you, tomorrow, sell the company you bought yesterday . . . on terms equal to or better than the deal you made?

Business buyers make a big mistake when they **misunderstand or underestimate** the **importance** of the difference between value and marketability.

Some kinds of businesses, even profitable ones, cannot be sold because of lack of marketability.

Who cares what somebody claims to be the value of a company if nobody wants to own it?

Why settle for some of the opportunities?

Wouldn't you like to access the *entire* market of businesses for sale? How about the unadvertised businesses quietly for sale by-owner? And the companies that could be for sale if you inquire the right way?

Everyone knows that brokers represent sellers.

But not everyone knows that broker listings fall far short of what's available. To see the rest, searchers must access the hidden market.

Go to my website to access the hidden market.

That's where you can find, depending upon the size and industry, up to 80% of the sellers.

Don't get me wrong: Buyers can benefit by purchasing businesses listed by brokers. But what do you do when brokers don't represent what you want to buy? You can wait . . . or you can access the hidden market.

But no matter where you find sellers, pay your own advisory team. Experts without any conflict-of-interest.

What about buyer competition?

No matter how adept at negotiating, your power is diluted when you compete with other buyers.

How much can buyers afford to lose?

Negotiating is about buyers and sellers trying to protect their downside and maximize their upside, isn't it?

So, what are we talking about? Here are some realities:

At least 10% is the reduction of the seller's asking price for buyers who **competently** analyze, value, and negotiate . . . especially if they're not bidding against other buyers. And that's not all. The discount can be **much** more for well-prepared buyers.

The purchase price and all the other terms **may not be the most important part**. There's something more important: It's the **quality** of the business. Its **sustainable** competitive advantages. It's the **environment** in which the company has and will operate. It's the **quality** of earnings.

It's a good idea to negotiate based on what's ahead instead of yesterday. Isn't it?

Lost opportunity cost is the money buyers give up, which is what they would have earned, had they sooner bought a business. And don't forget the depletion of savings for buyers who don't have an income while trying to buy a business. Time is money.

Reality: It's rare for the sellers' **asking** price, and other terms of sale, to be as REASONABLY good as they could be for buyers.

So . . . the answer is "no" if you don't ask.

According to business broker Jonathan Swanson: "The average business sale transaction falls apart 7 times before closing takes place."

Buyers who know how to process and negotiate suffer fewer deals falling through.

What you're reading can help you achieve done deals sooner with less aggravation. That's what you want, isn't it?

The bad news is most searchers don't have a clue. They simply don't know what they don't know; nor are they aware of the talent confronting them across the dealmaking tables.

Searching for businesses to buy can be frustrating. But it doesn't have to be . . . if searchers deploy best practices to handle their initial communications and interactions with brokers, sellers, and business owners.

Successful negotiators do what it takes to **understand everyone** on the other side of the table.

Searchers must avoid being hamstrung by their own constraints and biases; your advisory team can help you with this.

And the sooner people know what they need to know, the sooner the negotiating tide . . . turns in their favor.

Roleplay.

One of the most important things I do with buyers is to **roleplay** the kinds of interactions they're going to have with sellers and brokers. You get better results when you rehearse. But beware: Practicing with brokers and sellers can be self-defeating.

Guess what? Why do you think brokers, owners and sellers **read my how-to books written for buyers**? They're getting a heads up about how well-informed buyers will interact with them. This is what I mean by understanding the other side of the dealmaking table . . . **before** you venture onto the playing field.

Since we're talking about perception and behavior, let's talk about **buyer fever**.

Buyer fever.

Many mistakes business buyers make are errors of omission, not knowing what to do. Even people who know what to do sometimes do the wrong thing, especially if they have a bad case of BUYER FEVER – wanting a particular business so badly they suspend their common sense.

What can cause a fatal case of buyer fever?

How many of these 10 mistakes will you avoid?

1. Buyer competition, real or phony. Competition will increase your temperature.

2. Deciding upon your acquisition criteria after you commence your search.

3. Advisory team is infected by conflict-of-interest.

4. Inadequate due diligence.

5. Being unaware of the selling prices and terms of sale for similar businesses.

6. Weak-kneed negotiating. Being too-easily influenced by the seller and seller representatives.

7.   Using "good luck" business valuation techniques.

8.   Unenforceable verbal representations or understandings.

9.   Non-definitive purchase agreement.

10. Premature closing/completion.

Those mistakes can cause buyer fever because it's what you don't know that can harm you.

You don't have to buy what's offered to you.

Buyers knowing *how* to search don't worry about losing opportunities. Worthwhile deals are like buses; more will be by soon.

Let's consider 6 styles of negotiating.

- Darwinism

- Disco Ball

- Fastball

- Hardball

- Softball

- Dodgeball

The amount and kind of motivation of brokers and sellers determines your styles for negotiating. Most buyers deploy all these styles.

YOUR motivation, too, comes into play. Why ARE you looking for an acquisition?

Darwinism

What does **Darwinism** and buying a business have in common?

Pardon me for being crude . . . but it comes down to eat or be eaten.

Searchers who don't work harder and smarter are going to be . . . (you choose):

- taken advantage of, and/or

- be beaten out of or be too late for the best deals grabbed by competing buyers.

Disco Ball

By Disco Ball I mean the bright and shiny opportunity. Advertising clickbait, like what you see on websites such as bizbuy-sell.com. Or maybe it's the business-for-sale offering profile.

Yes. It can be bright and shiny, the best news ever! Too bad it's rarely reality.

Fastball

Use fastball to create or sustain urgency.

Time is of the essence. Let's get it done!

Moving ahead quickly *can* work . . . but it also exposes everyone to shallow thinking and missteps.

I like to deploy fastballs when it appears the other side is losing attention or is distracted.

Use fastball to refresh brokers and sellers that you're seriously interested in moving forward. "So, let's get going." And then you can (and probably should) s-l-o-w it down.

Hardball

Some sellers present unrealistic offerings. (Right?) They browbeat you to quickly evaluate the company for sale. They tell you other buyers are hovering. They say, **"Move quickly or move aside!"**

Some sellers shop your offer to other buyers hoping to create a bidding war. Another trick is the good-cop bad-cop ploy where the broker and seller double-team you, keeping you *involved* but off-balance.

But don't fear buyers. You, too, have a responding hardball tactic: It's called the walk away.

Sellers also deploy the walk away tactic. Think carefully about your demands and how you present them . . . and what you are willing to trade to get what you want.

Hardball negotiating **may or may not** work in the buyer's favor. It's more confrontational than collaborative.

But right now, write down this word: "Slapback."

Expect responses in kind.

Which means a returning ball thrown HARD.

Belittling and bluffing are two of the most common things buyers do when they're playing hardball.

Belittling is not smart.

Bluffing: Well . . . it can be powerfully dangerous or dangerously powerful!

Some people are infamous for demanding unreasonable concessions. When it works, it may be good for them. But they better be able to afford it when people reject ultimatums. Can you afford to lose the deal?

So, instead of starting your negotiation with a lowball offer, keep the ball in play. Privately compute the reasonable range of value for the company you might buy. And then begin by offering terms at the low end of the range.

The seller probably won't keep talking to you unless you show written and reasonable evidence for your initial offer.

Sweeten the pie by telling the seller that the price could go up if, during due diligence, you can prove the seller's claims and if you see growth for the company.

Later, you can adjust the price up or down as you discover more about the company and its owner.

Negotiating by a thousand cuts can be smarter than a take-it-or-leave it initial offer.

So, what's the lesson here? **Not properly** playing hardball can win skirmishes but abort the deal.

Hardball negotiating tactics can signal that the hardballer has no better argument to make, no worthwhile counter proposal.

Don't let your hardball tactics be perceived by the other side as your last and unconvincing playing card.

Hardball negotiating is usually a last resort. It can be used infrequently on the way to a win-win deal. But carefully. Sometimes . . . there's no going back when you offend brokers and sellers.

Softball

Ever hear the phrase Steel Magnolia? It's a woman with the strength of steel, yet the gentleness of a magnolia. Her smile makes you want more. But don't get caught trying to take advantage. Ouch!

We should rephrase *softball*. Let's call it *seemingly* softball. This is one of my favorites. It's like judo, where you convert someone's push into your momentum.

Seemingly softballing is delivered with steel backing your gentle effort. It's how you and sellers can establish and preserve your healthy and collaborative relationship.

Everyone is keeping their eye on their expected outcome: A win-win done deal.

Dodgeball

Do you have an unblinking eye over the entire playing field? Can you see and anticipate what's coming?

The better you prepare, the better you'll see.

It's human for all of us to take our eyes off the ball . . . even, sometimes, when it's most important to see what's coming.

One of the most important things I can do for my clients is to help look after their self-interest when they're distracted or when they're not seeing reality.

BTW, do-it-yourselfers are especially penalized when they're blindsided.

Remember the 5 Ds of dodgeball:

- Dodge

- Duck

- Dip

- Dive

- Dodge again.

Dodge ball works best when people don't know you're playing it.

Use it to avoid taking a stand, to divert attention, to distract. . . when someone is trying to get you to do something that you're not ready to handle.

Answering questions with questions is dodgeballing!

Winning Relationships

Let's switch from styles of negotiating to the condition that fosters win-win done deals:

Friendly, honest, trusting, harmonious relationships among the people around the dealmaking table.

I'm talking about building healthy rapport.

A big tip: Detach people from disagreements.

Don't take it personally!

And, please, no insults or eyerolling at sellers!

Look to the evidence.

Not enough evidence? Ask for it.

Simply asking for evidence focuses on the information, not the personalities.

People either have convincing evidence or they don't.

Gently walk away from *irrational* people. But leave the door open. Sometimes sellers recognize reality and then come back. But they'll be reluctant to do it if you slam the door in their face.

Evidence can be found in the articles published by industry trade journals. You'll see the vulnerabilities and opportunities associated with the industry. The articles identify industry consultants and other resources whom you can contact for additional information. Use the Internet, too.

Other evidence is in the **Annual Statement Studies** from the Risk Management Association. You'll see current and historical financial ratios for most industries. So, when the seller says the company's numbers are wonderful, you can *tactfully* reply, "Not according to your industry averages."

More evidence for negotiations you can get from databases publishing **statistics about done deals**. Not merely the selling prices, but some of the other terms of the transactions.

Industry reports are available from IBISWorld, one of several purveyors of enlightening information.

You can even find Concentration Ratios by industry sectors, from the **Economic Censuses**. It's a ratio that indicates the size of firms in relation to their industry.

Why is knowing this important?

Too many buyers acquire companies having too much competition.

It's essential to have a realistic context within which to evaluate opportunities and detect vulnerabilities. **Isn't it?**

Another big tip: Focus on mutual benefits.

Instead of W.I.I.F.M., think about what's in it for US.

Keep asking: What can we do to keep the ball moving toward a win-win deal? What alternatives can we consider? How do the terms of the deal we're arguing about compare to other buy/sell transactions?

Negotiating IS competing.

And it doesn't have to be unfair. It can be a friendly interchange where everyone wants a fair deal and is willing to collaborate and compromise to get it.

Tactics for win-win deals.

Let's think about the interactions between buyers, brokers, and sellers.

It begins by preparing for dealmaking.

Your tactics must align with your strategy.

Strategy is in your Business Buyer Marketing Plan.

Don't show brokers and sellers your Business Buyer Marketing Plan.

If you don't have one, I can help you create a WINNING Business Buyer Marketing Plan.

If your search is not working well-enough for you, go to my website and sign up for my Searcher and Search Evaluation.

Let's, now, consider your communicating and negotiating **tactics**.

Searchers who don't fully-understand the buy/sell playing field give away advantages to brokers and sellers.

I'm not kidding when I tell you that the typical buyer puts about as much effort into researching the best way to find and buy businesses as people research toasters to buy. Business purchases, like toasters, can be around for a long time. Buy in haste. Regret at leisure.

Benchmarking is first, and it is key.

Benchmarking is where we **begin** on the playing field. We go to websites like bizbuysell.com. We discover, compare, and make note of the offerings of businesses for sale. We're not yet responding to the offerings. We want to see how they stack up against similar and other kinds of businesses for sale.

We're collecting comparative data about the brokers and sellers making the offers. We can learn a lot about how brokers do what they do. This helps us focus on what appear to be the most transparent and fair-dealing brokers. And we red-flag brokers who hide the ball from us. Why waste time with brokers and sellers who are **not** forthcoming with the kinds of info buyers need?

One of the most important research tasks is to check out pricing multiples and sales pitches. Also, the financial and nonfinancial info published about businesses for sale.

- Multiples, pitches, financial and nonfinancial.

My webpage shows how to do it: What the Smartest Business Buyers Do First.

Evaluate the marketplace, too.

Go beyond collecting information about asking and selling prices. Evaluate what's happening in the industries of the customers and suppliers upon which the company depends.

Don't keep it to yourself!

Show sellers your research findings about the company and its industry . . . **if** it will help you make your case. At the least, sharing shows the seller that you're seriously interested in the industry . . . therefore, it's up to the owner to sell you on the company for sale.

You're not the only one preparing.

Everyone Googles. You Googled me, didn't you? Brokers, sellers, and owners Google you before they agree to meet you. And later they Google again to discover what you haven't told them.

Your online presence must nicely showcase you.

Buyers do better if they, upfront, get guidance and support from an expert-negotiator . . . especially an advisor who every day helps **buyers** interact with brokers and sellers.

A pro without conflict-of-interest. Someone whose loyalty is to you. Only to you. BTW, I'm applying for the job.

Initial interactions with brokers and sellers.

It's what you do first, and how you do it, that determines your results. There's no margin for error. No second chances.

Negotiations begin with establishing friendly and trusting relationships. **Likeability** smooths the inevitable bumpy pathways ahead.

Be assertive. Not confrontational. Be tactful and apparently flexible . . . but not overly accommodating.

Communicate directly with the decision-makers.

All of them at the same time. Otherwise, you're going to hear a lot of, "I'll get back to you after I talk to so-and-so," which is a great ploy for sellers to gain negotiating advantages.

Sellers of good companies are rarely stupid.

A good way for you to be dumped with no right of return is to be obnoxious or unreasonably indecisive.

Everything is negotiable.

If you can't get what you want, get something else from another element of negotiation. It's about balancing.

Everyone's always negotiating.

I'll say it again: **Everyone's** always negotiating!

It may not feel like it to you. And you certainly don't want brokers and sellers detecting the subtle ways *you* influence *them* more than they influence you.

And for that to happen you need to **discover** upfront **why** the company is for sale, what **motivates** the seller and what the seller and broker **expect** to get from you. Carefully make note of what you see and hear. It **will** change as you proceed with them.

Don't be too quick to state your position. You'll go much further if you cause the other side talk about what **they will do** to achieve a win-win deal.

Talk before you write.

Discuss the alternatives, the obstacles, whatever bothers you **before** you put anything in writing with sellers and brokers. Once something becomes the written word it's not easy to retract it.

Silence pays.

Don't feel urgency to keep talking. Explain yourself in the fewest words and then shut up. Put the onus on the seller to respond. That's the nice thing about asking questions. Instead of saying, "I'll pay **this** price for your business," you could say, "Would such and such price be acceptable to you? And then ask, "Why not?"

Never forget cashflow while negotiating.

Don't use all your available cash or borrowing power for the purchase. Retain cash reserves and credit lines for working capital and contingencies.

The price is more important to sellers.

Don't forget that price is more important to the seller than it *should* be to you. At the beginning, do **not** scare away sellers by objecting to or challenging their asking price. Many sellers will lower their price later if they trust and like you, if they think you will take care of their employees and their "baby."

Don't lose sight of the fact that you want to control the business and its cash flow. You can use creative purchase terms to justify paying a higher price than what you want to pay. But don't be stupid.

Would another buyer go for the same deal if you must sell the business shortly after you buy it?

Do not pay for profit you create.

Do not pay an inflated price for profit you will create that is higher than historical profit. (An exception *might* be a business that is poised for a big windfall or when it makes sense to pay the seller based on an earnout.)

Don't pay for skim.

Skimming is prevalent in some fields. When recasting profit and budgeting cash flow, it's **not** a best practice to include the seller's admission of income not reported to revenue or income taxing authorities. The seller effectively received part of his price in the form of taxes not paid. He lied to the government. Would he lie to you?

Negotiating is not for sissies.

It's also not for first timers. No matter how nicely people behave, negotiating is like making sausage. It's not for the faint of heart; it **is** messy; sometimes disgusting.

If you want to crater a deal, hire a lousy negotiator, which (pardon me) might include yourself. And probably does for buyers and sellers who negotiate directly with each other.

Write this down: Who will wear the black hat when something unpleasant must be said? Do you want to be blamed for it? Wouldn't it be better to blame someone else, such as a member of your advisory team?

Ungluing sticky negotiations.

There's only one thing more important than knowing how to negotiate. It's knowing how to prepare yourself and then find worthwhile businesses. That's why I wrote the book: *How to Prepare Yourself and Find the Right Business to Buy.*

The dilemma for buyers and sellers is balancing risk and value. Nobody wants to feel that they've been had. Nor do they want to lose good opportunities. Keep this in mind: See how both sides of the potential deal perceive balancing *their* risk and value. Negotiators who are aware of this dilemma are more likely to achieve agreements.

Let's say you really want to own the sellers' company. But the seller won't agree with your offer. One way you can resume control is to let the seller know his company is competing with another opportunity that seriously interests you. This can increase your leverage, and it causes some sellers to say, "go for it!"

Therefore, if you've already decided you want to own the company, it's too dangerous to mention competition. You'll still have your other opportunity if this deal falls through.

Instead of hardballing the seller, how about nourishing your relationship? Focusing on the good news; what you have in common. Both of you like the company; it's something you have in common, so play to it.

Help the seller experience marketplace reality . . . and *your* perspective:

"I really like what you've done with your company . . . and how it will feel for me to grow it and extend your legacy. But your proposal does not provide me with enough return on investment. Can we consider that for a while?"

Here is where you introduce what your research has uncovered: The legitimate asking and selling price multiples for similar businesses.

And compare the company's financial ratios with industry averages.

Encourage the seller to build the bridge to span the distance between your disagreement:

Another tactic is to ask for advice: "I trust you and I want to rely upon your knowledge of your business and its industry. What do I need to know to see . . . like you do . . . the value of your company?"

Lay the cards on the table. Rank their importance to you and sellers.

- Ask: "What are the issues, the obstacles to our agreement?"

- Move them around on the table, each of you prioritizing them.

- Talk about relative risk. And the reality or probability of fearsome issues.

- How do the respective priorities differ? Can you see any ways to exchange benefits?

First, resolve the easiest, least important issues, and then move on to the difficulties.

You can't have it all your way. And neither can sellers. Help sellers understand this.

BTW, this is where advisory teams can build bridges . . . or not.

Negotiate; don't compromise.

"When you have a disagreement, *negotiating* a solution works best." That's according to experts Rob Pascale and Lou Primavera.

"To be clear, *negotiation* is not compromise. In a *negotiation*, each person gets something in exchange for giving something the other person wants. In *compromise*, neither person gets what they want. They often settle on some middle ground between two ends of an issue, with the result that neither is satisfied with the solution."

"Negotiated solutions work much better than compromises on a lot of levels. Each person gets something they really want in exchange for giving something the other person really wants."

Go slow to go fast.

Negotiate in haste. Regret at leisure.

Think about when you wished you did **not** rush it.

Take time to identify and evaluate the seller's *emotional* issues, not merely what pertains to the company and the deal.

Slowing down the interactions with brokers and sellers can calm emotion, improve rapport and trust.

If you have other potential deals on the table (which you should), sometimes going slowly motivates sellers to make concessions for fear of losing you. But don't be a ditherer or unreasonable. Stall carefully. Invoking a higher authority is one way to do it: "I have to run that by so-and-so."

The higher authority.

Let someone else, such as someone on your advisory team, wear the black hat or give you resource material to which you refer when you present your case to sellers. Use the ploy to buy time, gain concessions and get advice from your advisors.

Most buyers who try to negotiate directly with a seller offend the seller or make unnecessary concessions. An experienced negotiator, working on behalf of the buyer, can benefit the buyer.

Don't fall for higher authority.

If the seller won't provide information or answers because he says it is out of his control, demand to speak directly to whoever is in control of the issue(s). Don't let the "confidential" relationship between the business and other parties stop you from digging for the truth. Otherwise, you might suffer the "con" in confidentiality.

Risky legal documents foisted on naïve searchers.

NDAs, letters of interest, letters of intent, offers to purchase. These are the obvious ones. My advice to buyers is this: Have your attorney prepare these before you deploy each of them. Don't wait for the other side to hand you're their document. Tell your legal counsel you need boilerplate that you can use with numerous sellers, merely filling in the blanks pertaining to each offering.

The money you invest to control the legal docs, assuming you have the right counsel, can protect your downside, speed up dealmaking and maximize your opportunity.

Talk to me if you want to know the best way to identify worthwhile advisors, especially legal, accounting, tax, and valuation. I've seen all the pitches and many of the disasters.

Care and feeding of taxation and legal counsel.

Be the first to draft your contract of purchase. Don't believe me? Want to accept that nicely printed boilerplate contract foisted on you? Talk to a lawyer about this. Ask about who gets the advantages and who will spend more money on legal and accounting fees.

Don't be surprised if much of the business' value diminishes in the "eleventh hour," which usually arises as your legal and tax counsel are wrapping up their work for closing or completion of your deal.

Don't assume you can back out of the deal or renegotiate it. Savvy sellers or lawyers can force you to perform the purchase contract, which means you might get less than what you bargained for.

When is the most opportune time to hire tax and legal counsel? It's too late if due diligence is done, or if financing is pending and you have informally agreed with the seller in principle on most of the terms of purchase. It's time for the purchase agreement. Oops! Bad move!

Hire the right kind of tax and legal counsel the right way and no later than when you begin due diligence on a deal you **expect** to make.

One of the things I like to do with my clients is to help them devise a list of discussion points that they use to interview legal counsel and then later delve into more deeply with legal counsel. Ask your attorney or solicitor to give you tips, such as what risks to detect an avoid and what benefits or concessions are likely to come up during negotiations that PRECEDE the preparation of a definitive purchase agreement.

Ask your lawyer what you should be thinking about with respect to contingencies, covenants, and holdbacks. Google those words if they're not clear to you.

Have a backup attorney if your primary one drops the ball or is not available when you need advice or documents. This happens. Believe me.

There's something more important than tangible assets.

Tangible assets are important, but the value of a business is influenced more by its intangibles such as its sustainable competitive advantages and its goodwill.

Remember: Goodwill is the *excess* price you pay to buy a company greater its fair market value.

Make a mistake valuing a **tangible** asset and you pay more than it's worth.

Overvalue **goodwill** and you make a **bad investment**.

Dormant and actual risks among employees.

Interview key employees!

With the seller's advance written permission.

Buyers start in second gear when they take over a company with disgruntled employees.

One of the major reasons why so many buyers suffer bad deals is their failure to adequately investigate small and midsize companies for sale . . . **from the perspective of a *company insider*.**

The employees of companies for sale can be the buyer's best reality check.

You can discover the real reason for sale. What you discover can materially improve negotiations.

Probe key employees for business and industry intelligence, which you can use to manage the business or buy and manage another company.

Own or Lease? Real Property/Real Estate.

Don't mingle valuation for business and real estate.

It's a good idea to separately price real property from the business opportunity. Employ a well-qualified, independent real estate appraiser for the property and another well-qualified appraiser to value the company.

Valuation aside, there are good reasons not to purchase the real estate with the company.

One reason you don't want to own the real estate the down payment you make takes dilutes the cash you have to buy the company.

And debt service will eat your cash flow. *And* the promissory note or mortgage will adversely affect your balance sheet.

Moreover, if things go wrong, it's better to be delinquent on rent due to somebody else.

Don't tell the seller upfront you don't want the real estate. Later, when you negotiate for the business, show the seller why it's smarter for him to sell the real property to a third-party investor from whom you lease space. This can be a simple item to arrange if you properly communicate it to the seller.

You can purchase a much larger and safer company if you use your money to buy the business, period.

Premises lease.

Get a copy of the lease. Detect pitfalls early . . . surprises later will be costly. You might not be able to talk to the landlord early during due diligence, but you must nail down several risks, and ask the seller how s/he will help mitigate the risks. Keep a record of this discussion.

Assumption of the lease. Assignment. Pricing. Duration. Personal guarantee.

What's the market rate for the lease that you'll have to assume if the business must remain at its location? You may not be able to negotiate a better deal with the landlord, but you can make it up with the some of the other terms you agree to pay for the business.

Keep in mind that lenders and investors require the lease duration to be at least as long as the financing to buy the business.

And, if you intend to protect the location or sell the company down the road, there must be enough remaining time on the lease.

The walk-away.

Let's first consider the contingencies. Things we may not like but can try to do something about them. The walk-away is always at our command.

If you've been on the playing field talking to brokers and sellers, you have or you will encounter bullies, liars, and unappetizing situations through which you must bravely go to have a chance of evaluating businesses for sale.

Negotiating with bullies.

"Giving in rarely makes them stop wanting more," says lawyer and mediator Bill Eddy. Here are three tips from the article:

- Know Your Bottom Line

- Appear Calm and Patient

- Bring in a Neutral Decision-Maker or Mediator

"Get support, know your bottom line, get an advocate to help you negotiate."

And here's my two cents for handling bullies: Intimidate!

Intimidation is powerful—use it as a last resort on friendly brokers and sellers. Don't make empty threats, especially to bullies; they might call your bluff.

Negotiating with liars.

I'm not alleging that sellers are liars. In fact, the saying is: "Buyers are liars."

I know. "Liar" is a nasty word. So, let's add some PC. How about misrepresentation or deception?

What I'm saying is you'll probably interact with liars, and you may not know it. But if you are, here are a few tips from negotiating expert, Dale Hartley:

- Forewarned is forearmed

- Set your priorities

- Focus on what you can control

- Quid Pro Quo

- Ask: "What will YOU do if I do not purchase one today?"

The advice above aligns with what I've been telling my clients since the 1970s, which is to ask EVERYONE they interview:

"Is there any information that you have not disclosed to me that might have an adverse bearing on the viability or the value of the business for sale?"

And, when all else fails to go your way . . . walk away.

Reps and warranties.

A business buying joke: Depend upon the seller's reps and warranties.

Don't rely on reps and warranties without good reasons.

Ask your legal counsel for a list and brief description of the most important ones. Ask for a realistic assessment of the post-closing/completion contractual protections provided by reps and warranties. To what degree should business buyers investigate the kinds of issues reflected in the reps and warranties section of buy/sell agreements?

You will save lots of aggravation and money if you tactfully inquire early during your conversations with brokers and sellers about the likely representations and warranties. And certainly, during due diligence. What you discover will be highly useful to you during negotiations, and what you learn may cause you to wisely abort the potential deal.

Negotiating reps and warranties is about apportioning risk.

Buyers want sellers to guarantee just about anything the buyer or legal counsel can dream up, which might become a contingency or risk . . . especially post-closing.

Sellers want to be fully cashed out at closing, with no trailing contingencies.

It doesn't much matter what buyers and sellers want. What matters is what they're willing to risk making their deal. And this is where you better have an advisory team with savvy and reasonable expectations, which are aligned with yours, to help everyone facilitate deals that should occur.

Look into reps and warranties insurance.

Don't be overly-comforted by the reps and warranties in purchase contracts. What if whatever the stated recourse cannot be achieved?

Listen to my interviews of M&A legal counsel, which you'll find on my YouTube channel: https://www.youtube.com/TedLeveretteTheBusinessBuyerAdvocate

Due diligence.

Don't prematurely take a stand, challenging the owner. The more time you spend in the business the more intelligence you can collect about the industry. You can discover the best customers, suppliers, and industry experts. Even alternative sources of financing. You may not do the deal you're examining but it'll help you do deal you do.

You can derive your own due diligence questions based on your research. And if it doesn't work for you, hire an experienced advisor. How about me?

What won't work is to pester sellers and brokers with irrelevant questions, or poorly crafted questions and requests. They won't put up with it.

Warren Buffett says the most important thing he looks for when evaluating a company is its "sustainable competitive advantage."

Ask this: What are the specific elements of your company's competitive advantage, and how, specifically, do they pay off for you in the marketplace?

This topic reminds me of the adage: You can put lipstick on a pig but it's still a pig. Don't fall for superficial answers or the promise of recent cosmetic changes to the company. Watch out for sellers who attempt to disguise the true nature of their company and its marketplace.

Holdbacks and adjustments at closing.

Post-closing risks and liabilities are a big concern for buyers and sellers.

The key points I'm making come from a banker, Louie Jachim of Northwest Bank.

M&A transactions contain a holdback defined in the Purchase & Sale Agreement. It's a portion of the purchase price that is not paid to the seller at closing, but rather held in a third-party escrow account. The funds held back can offer both parties a degree of comfort that funds will be available to mitigate potential post-closing risks. Typical escrow accounts, as a percentage of the total purchase price, are 10-15%.

Here are a few examples:

- Post-Closing Purchase Price Adjustments: Frequently referred to as "Net Working Capital Adjustments," these contingencies focus on the assets and liabilities of the selling company, which change because of normal operations between the time both parties agreed on an original purchase price and the closing date. These amounts may be substantial depending on length of time between agreement and execution.

- Indemnification Holdback for Representations and Warranties

- Specifically Identified Liability

- Earn-Out Provisions

Raising the ante and knowing when to fold 'em.

Raising the ante . . . the answer is "no" if you don't ask.

Reality: It's rare for the sellers' asking price, and other terms of sale, to be as REASONABLY good as they could be for buyers.

When "no" is better than "yes." Make "Nos" happen. Yes, I'm suggesting that you reasonably do whatever it takes to hear "No, I don't want to do that" or "I cannot accept your proposal."

Remember, the seller's asking price is just that. Asking. Sellers expect you to say "no" and then propose a lower price . . . don't they?

Buyers who don't hear "no" during negotiations are not asking for enough. Don't leave money on the table. Get to "no" to get to "yes." Respectfully!

Another kind of "no" means "no-way" so I'm taking the highway outta here!

The article, "Negotiators Are Motivated to Agree," suggests: "The best outcome is not always reaching an agreement. Some people believe that reaching an agreement is an important part of negotiating. They treat a negotiation as a failure if they do not reach an agreement, even if each party does better by walking away from the table than they would by accepting the best agreement."

Successfully buying a business means you get what you want for what you're willing to give. Searchers, such as my clients, who know how to find a continuous stream of worthwhile opportunities walk away from the best of the mediocre deals.

(Sometimes) answer questions with questions.

But what about when brokers and sellers do it to you? Besides switching you from your agenda to theirs, people who don't adequately answer your questions might be hiding a deficiency, which if it becomes known to you can cause you to walk away.

Don't disclose your time constraints, which has to do with your deadlines. This will be used against you!

Get explicit answers to your questions before you say something you shouldn't. Don't permit question-dodging.

And, of course, answer questions with questions when it can benefit you.

One of the most valuable things I do for my clients is to help them interpret and deploy the strategies and tactics I explain in my how-to books, webinars, and other things.

Remember the advice from Vincent Lombardi: "Only perfect practice makes perfect."

One of the most important things I do with buyers is to **ro-leplay** the kinds of interactions they're going to have with sellers and brokers. You get better results when you rehearse. But beware: Practicing with brokers and sellers can be self-defeating.

Please follow up with me so I can help you deploy the insights I've shared with you. Preferably before you communicate with brokers and sellers.

Propose respectfully.

Everybody wants to avoid loss of face. Takedowns don't work if you want to buy the right business the right way.

If you're not a good listener don't bother going onto the deal-making playing field.

Don't disappear.

Be available throughout your evaluation and negotiation. Make it easy to keep the play in motion and moving toward where you want it to go.

Controls the location to control the negotiations.

Not always true, but true enough to get your attention, right now. You can learn more reading this article, "When Negotiating, Does Location Matter?"

Negotiate in your location or a neutral one. Ever hear about the home team advantage?

"The researchers found those negotiating in their home territory outperformed the visitors regardless of whether they were purchasers or sellers in the negotiation."

And by location I include email. Sometimes it makes sense to exchange email if you want the other side to have time to think about your proposal or if you want time to think about what's proposed to you. Face-to-face is not always best, especially if the other side is evasive or a "fast-talker" adept at manipulating people.

Good mood — Not so good — Angry.

Especially at the beginning it's essential that you demonstrate that you're in a good mood, and you're expecting to feel better on your way to a win-win deal.

But you don't want to appear to be a chump, do you? No. So, when the other side says or does something you do *not* like, such as making a ridiculous statement or proposal, frown. Pause. Don't overplay it.

You're disappointed and they need to know it. And by silently pausing they might blurt out something better.

Similarly, don't be afraid to get mad when people abuse you.

Don't leave meetings without scheduling the next event.

It might be another meeting to exchange or discuss more data. Or it might be agreeing on the deadline to complete a task. Keep the play in motion.

Email key points from your conversation.

You might as well find out right now if what you think occurred is consistent with what's in their minds. Misunderstandings are like mosquito bites. The longer it takes to treat them, the more they itch, the more you scratch and the more you bleed.

What searchers should disclose, how and when.

Minimal commitment-maximum protection

This controversial, so think carefully:

Strive in your initial communications (including documents you submit to brokers and sellers) to convey minimum information and commitment necessary to satisfy the other side of the dealmaking table and to maximum the protections of yourself.

That's what brokers and sellers do, don't they?

Proceed like peeling an onion. Be more definitive as you go along but don't put the cart before the horse.

This is a good topic to discuss with your attorney, including the typical business issues and procedural things that are likely to nourish (or discourage) win-win friendly relationships with sellers and (maybe) brokers.

Brokers are less likely to cooperate. Many of them try to coerce buyers into legal documents whose intent and content is premature or worse.

Which is why I encourage my clients to find businesses for sale by-owner.

Disclosing your financial statement.

Savvy buyers know how to present their personal financial capability.

This is one of the most important topics I cover with people who sign up for my Searcher and Search Evaluation. Here's a preview:

Show too much, you increase the probability that you'll pay too much and make a larger than necessary down payment.

Reveal too little, you won't get a chance to evaluate the company.

Don't reveal your financial situation without first getting a signed NDA from anyone who will see your financial statement.

Don't show your entire net worth.

And that's it for now.

Whoever says it in fewest words wins. ™ (I coined that phrase.)

But not this one: "*Whoever speaks next loses.*" I discovered that in a LinkedIn article by **David Bennett**. He explains:

"When you are in the throes of working on a deal and you get to the critical points, you simply stop talking. You simply hold back and let things be. You are not to oversell your point or undermine yours or the other persons position."

Let the other side fill in the silence. They might negotiate with themselves; asking questions, making concessions; offering a better deal.

Don't be a weasel.

- Get to the point.

- Don't cry. (I'm kidding, No, I'm serious. Are you smiling?)

- Don't shove things under the rug. Address whatever comes up when it does. Which, sometimes, means agreeing with the other side that you will sideline the issue until a specific date or event arises.

- Don't unnecessarily evade; say what you mean and want . . . and mean it.

- Cut the manipulation, the stalling, the dancing around issues.

- Respond with what they ask for . . . or say no. And then maybe, suggest an alternative.

- Instead of saying "well . . . I'll think about it" say "let's think about that right now, together."

- Replace "not exactly" with exactly, which means definitively ask for what you want or are willing to give.

- Avoid irrelevancy. When they inject something irrelevant, say "I'm having trouble seeing the relevancy. Can you show me why that's important for us?"

- You will make better deals if your language and demeanor is direct and confident.

- Don't hedge your meanings with weasel actions or words.

And don't let them weasel you!

Who makes the first offer?

If you're shopping online and with brokers, mostly sellers lead with asking prices and terms.

The hidden market of *unadvertised by-owner* sellers differs. Most owners don't know how to price their company for sale.

According to Adam D. Galinsky, writing for the Harvard Business School:

Common wisdom for negotiations says it's better to wait for your opponent to make the first offer. In fact, you may win by making the first offer yourself.

There's not enough time, now, for me to explain, so Google and then read the article: "When to Make the First Offer in Negotiations."

But here's a hint: "More often than not, negotiators who make first offers come out ahead."

"They set the tone for the negotiation. When we hear a first offer, we find ourselves pulled in that direction, and have trouble adjusting our own judgments." Psychologist Adam Grant.

Psychology and Marketing professor, Art Markman, elaborates: "It is probably a good idea to make the first offer. That initial offer serves as an anchor. However, after you make that initial offer, resist the temptation to give reasons to justify that initial bid. Instead, let the other party come back with a counteroffer. Chances are, that counteroffer will not be adjusted as far away from your initial offer as it would have been if you had made arguments in your own favor."

Lowering frustration while negotiating.

Negotiating won't be as frustrating if you know the lay of the land. It's less risky if you avoid risky situations.

By reviewing and comparing many businesses, you will sharpen your analysis and negotiating skills. You will also avoid being susceptible to buying a business because it appears to be the only one available.

Have several deals in analysis and negotiation.

The best negotiators can prevail over you without you realizing what's coming. Some mistakes can be fatal. Missteps can defer or lessen whatever benefit you seek.

Donald Trump says, "Sometimes your best investments are the ones you don't make."

Pricing/valuation nonsense.

Remember: Price isn't everything

The key is to get the seller to narrowly focus on what you want to offer, what you want to be influencing. What you're willing to trade for what you want to get.

In negotiation, buyers and sellers have some things the other side wants. Not "something." Some things! The key is to get the other side to narrowly focus on what you want to offer, what you want to be influencing. What you're willing to trade for what you want to get.

Savvy buyers, for example, pitch lots of benefits to sellers that go way beyond the purchase price. Sellers will trade some of their asking price for other benefits . . . for buyers who know how to showcase the alternatives.

Sellers who play hard to get can cause buyers to give up more than necessary.

What's Missing in EBITDA?

According to business appraiser, George Abraham: The challenge with EBITDA multiples is they are general in nature, and almost always contain a myriad of assumptions. Furthermore, they can be easily manipulated to suit the party using the multiple.

I think Warren Buffett says it best, "People who use EBITDA are either trying to con you or they're conning themselves." Charlie Munger, Buffett's right-hand man goes even further: "I think that every time you see the word EBITDA, you should substitute the word 'bullshit'."

Strong words from one of the most successful businessmen on the planet.

What about pricing?

The asking price rarely has anything to do with value.

Warren Buffett says: "It's far better to buy a wonderful company at a fair price, than a fair company at a wonderful price."

Even the best brokers are hogtied by some of the sellers they represent.

Give the other side a good reason to sell to you at a lower price, with less expensive financing or extend the term for installment payments.

If you want to buy at the lowest price, get a credible appraisal. It's the irrefutable remedy when sellers are motivated to sell but they don't like your offering price.

The seller's **asking** price is not the benchmark from which a wise buyer makes an offer to purchase. Successful business buyers make their initial offer from the perspective of an independent, competent estimate of the most probable range for the selling price. This s where your earlier research into asking prices and completed transactions comes in.

"Price is what you pay; value is what you get." Warren Buffett

Don't believe that sellers understand valuation.

The typical seller makes up his asking price. His basis is typically a high figure that a business broker mentioned; it might be what a similar business in another state sold for a few years ago or it simply feels right, given the blood, sweat, tears and money that the owner invested.

Educate the seller, even if he is represented by a business broker. Your *Business Buyer Advocate* can provide you with a credible *Ballpark Price Fairness Opinion*, which provides you with facts and logic. Use this knowledge to appeal to the seller's common sense. When and how you do so will take more explanation than I can explain today. Hint: Key is return on investment. What has been the seller's ROI? What will it be with the proceeds from the sale of the business? What will be your ROI and how does it compare to alternate investments?

Pricing assets.

Book value. Is it practical to ignore book value, replacing it with what it would cost to buy similar used equipment and fixtures? Why pay $1,000 book value for a used machine if you can buy it for $500. I had a client who told the seller: "You keep the equipment; I know where I can replace it for about half what you say it's worth, and have it delivered and working within a couple of days of closing."

How to cut through the valuation nonsense.

Would you like to cut through the "valuation" nonsense from brokers and sellers?

Access reliable statistics about the asking prices, sales prices, and terms of sale for the kinds, sizes, and locations of "comparable" businesses. Numerous third-party (i.e., independent) databases report this kind of data. Don't rely on the opinion of any single source of valuation or pricing.

The easiest way for brokers and sellers to "get real" about valuation is to show facts to them. Of course, some people don't want to be confused by the facts. In which case you can move on to another potential deal.

What about valuing goodwill?

Don't conflate goodwill with good luck.

Beware of goodwill, especially if its basis is the **owner's** business relationships with the company's customers, employees, landlord, bank, and suppliers. To what degree can you reasonably expect to match or surpass the quality of the seller's? Watch out for dependency! Is the owner indispensable to the company?

"10 Hard-Bargaining Tactics & Negotiation Skills"

I'm not going to cover this. Google the title to see the suggestions coming from the Harvard Program on Negotiation.

Using questions to uncover the truth and get what you want.

And the truth may set you free . . . for negotiating advantages.

Don't ask yes-no questions. Ask open-ended questions.

These kinds of questions are useful on issues such as price, financing, transition assistance, interviewing employees, customers, suppliers, and landlords.

Don't buy the wrong business or buy the wrong way.

Some people are surprised to discover they bought the wrong business. You cannot fix what you don't know is wrong. Most problems, when adequately identified, can be fixed (at least to some degree).

Some people acquire the *right* business the *wrong* way, which can turn winners into losers.

A lousy purchase contract can undermine a good business.

This can happen if the buyer didn't think carefully about the integration into the business' culture with his or her personal skills and attitudes.

Other reasons include: Seasonality, cash flow volatility, business cycle, business life phase (startups risky; mature okay unless stale, losing competitive advantages).

Donald Trump says, "Sometimes your best investments are the ones you don't make."

When being second can put you in first place.

Typical business buyers, especially do-it-yourselfers and people whose advisory team is inadequate, rush to make offers. Too many of them make lowball offers. They usually don't know what they don't know, which means they don't have a good enough appreciation for the seller's company. And they don't know how to make their case to the seller and the seller's representatives. This is wonderful for you.

Whether they like it or not, sellers get a wakeup call when they reject the first buyer who submits an offer to purchase. Most owners are devastated when they reject an offer, even a lousy offer. Perhaps their broker is thinking or says, "I told you so" regarding the seller's offering.

So, if you show up second, and if you properly and nicely handle yourself, you awaken the seller's hopefulness about achieving a done deal.

They bogeyman in the seller's closet is this: The longer a company is for sale, the lower will be the selling price and the attractiveness of the terms of sale.

But buyers, sloppy thirds and fourths could mean you, too, should pass by the opportunity.

Answering questions with questions.

Have you noticed the best salespeople answer your questions with questions? It's good for them; not so much for you.

Besides switching you from your agenda to theirs, people who don't adequately answer your questions might be hiding a deficiency, which if it becomes known to you can cause you to walk away.

One of the most frequent things you might disclose is your time constraints, which has to do with your deadlines. This will be used against you!

Get explicit answers to your questions before you say something you shouldn't. Don't permit question-dodging.

And, of course, answer questions with questions when it can benefit you.

So . . . one of the most important things you must detect is how time will affect the other side of your dealmaking table.

Don't tell "the other side" how you'll improve the biz.

Don't tell sellers or business brokers how you will fix or improve your potential acquisition. Doing so may encourage the seller to keep the business until s/he makes these improvements, and then put it back on the market for a higher price.

Selling mistakes delighting buyers.

Business buyers can exploit these common business mistakes.

But first, let's give sellers a fair chance.

Sellers: If you want to quickly sell your company on the best price and terms, fix vulnerabilities before offering your company. The sooner the better. If you don't, your mistakes erode the value of your company and . . . they make you crazy, don't they?

Okay, buyers, back to you.

The good news is most business owners learn to live with most of these problems. Their day of reckoning is when you show up to evaluate their company for sale. Too bad for them that they missed their opportunity to maximize the marketability and value of their business. Now it's yours to exploit.

You will be able to buy it for less money and on better terms. Why? Two reasons.

First: Negotiating leverage: These kinds of mistakes repel quite a few buyers. This means you won't have to compete against as many buyers. Plus, the seller will have trouble explaining the vulnerabilities.

Second: Better return on your investment: Once you gain control of the company you can fix these vulnerabilities. This increases your profit and increases your ROI.

So, here are a few of the most common business mistakes that buyers exploit.

I'm referring to sellers that work from an . . .

- Incoherent business plan

They

- Underrate customer satisfaction

- Fail to use creative financing

- Inappropriately advertise or publicize

- Maintain improper inventory

- Wrongly price products or services

- Manage by committee

- They're blind to the competition

- They don't recognize key trends

Okay, I suspect that a few sellers and brokers are reading this, so let's not totally stack the deck in favor of business buyers.

Sellers, are you are like most business owners, too busy handling day-to-day activities and putting out fires?

You probably have not taken the time to look at your business for what it really is—examining the strengths that give you a competitive advantage, and the vulnerabilities that threaten your future. And to do this from the point of view of a potential source of financing or a future business buyer.

Well, that's another mistake.

J. Paul Getty famously said:

> *There are always opportunities through which you can profit*
> *handsomely if you only will recognize and seize them.*

So, whether you're the seller or buyer get an outsider's perspective of your business, and a three-dimensional (past, present, future) snapshot of your business.

Doing so can unlock the value in any kind or size of business. It widens and lengthens your perspective, so you can make better decisions regarding the business you own or want to buy.

Okay, back to buyers: Don't worry; enough sellers will ignore my advice, which means you can get a better deal.

The seller will be your partner for a while.

How much value to business buyers comes from the sellers' post-acquisition transitional assistance? It's a two-edged sword; it can spell the difference between the new owners' success and failure.

To what degree, post-acquisition, is there a correlation between the buyers' degree of success from their company in relation to the length of time or the quality of the business sellers' transitional assistance for the buyer?

According to **Bob Fariss**, whose experience includes business brokerage, franchising and business ownership, the companies he helped sell performed best, after their sale, were the businesses where the seller's post-acquisition on-the-job performance conveyed a material amount of value to the buyer and the company.

Business Intermediary, **Ron Buck**, on LinkedIn writes: "Great question—and highly dependent on the cycle time of the business (i.e., how long it takes for the new owner to see a full cycle of activities), other support available (like a franchisor in a franchise resale), and the buyer's experience in the industry. I have a company for sale that sells holiday products—it takes a whole year for the buyer to see a cycle, so in that case a long transition/consulting arrangement is critical. On the other hand, the 24-hour gym buyer just needs to see a couple of weeks of operations and a month-end reporting cycle to the franchisor. Another franchise that I've resold has an extensive two-week training before closing, then parks a trainer on-site for a week after closing, followed-up by monthly visits and being on call. In that case, the transition period is more critical from the customer relationship handoff perspective than an operational one. Finally, the transition period should be flexible and should be structured to clearly put the new buyer in charge. Going into it, many buyers often think they want the seller around longer, and then once they realize that for them to make the changes they want to make and get the employees to start coming to them for decisions, that maybe having the seller around after a while is getting a little old."

John Martinka, The Escape Artist *, says, "It depends on the business. Time isn't as important as quality. And, most importantly, have a transition plan set up prior to closing. Last summer a client told the seller he didn't need him anymore—on the second day. And he's doing great. One client wanted 180 days; I convinced him 90 was enough and, later, he said, "On the 91st day I was so glad he wasn't coming in."

The adage is 'you never want to buy a business where the owner does not want to stay around for less than six months. You also never want to buy a business where the owner wants to stay longer than six months!' Two months full time, two months part time and on-call thereafter can be best when the owner is retiring. The exception is a more technical business where the owner's know-how is critical to the business.

Savvy buyers carefully evaluate, during dealmaking, the sellers' willingness and capability to stay on for a while after closing, which effectively means the seller is, temporarily, a crucial business "partner." And then the buyers and sellers specify the transitional assistance in their sale and purchase agreement or the sellers consulting or employment agreement.

Keep in mind the likelihood of compatibility between you and the former owner(s). Consider your relative expectations, outside influences and commitments, vision for the company, timelines, operational topics, work ethics, and the company's exposure to liability for the seller's activities working in or for the company. What about the allocation of responsibilities and the terms thereof? What about reporting and accountability? Will the former owner be compensated by way of a salary or consulting agreement? What about profit sharing. Who will be the face and voice of the company? How will you and the seller handle unresolved issues when disagreements arise? How will you handle early termination of the seller's transitional assistance, especially if it is not working well for you? What blow-back might arise?

Negotiating the training and transition agreement.

What is a Transition Services Agreement (TSA)?

Peter J. F. Ferrari, a corporate lawyer with over half a billion dollars in transaction experience, explains: A TSA is a limited term outsourcing or servicing agreement, generally between a Purchaser and a Seller, with the purpose of providing a smooth transition without stoppages or interruptions while the Purchaser is trying to integrate the purchased business into its operations. These agreements are generally entered into as part of an acquisition of a business or business unit and at the request of the Purchaser.

In smaller, owner-operated, turnkey transactions this type of agreement is often referred to as a Training and Transition Agreement.

Don't tell brokers what shouldn't be known to sellers.

The broker has a fiduciary obligation to obtain the best deal possible for the seller, at your expense. Don't blame the broker for doing his job. Use discretion when talking to brokers and sellers.

Ask for reasonably more than you expect.

Professional negotiators know it is effective to overstate demands. Doing so raises the perceived ceiling, which of course you will lower in return for something you truly want. On the other hand, be suspicious of sellers who are too amenable to your requests during due diligence and dealmaking. There is supposed to be a struggle, mild as it may be. The name of the game is pushing to near deadlock and then backing off, so you don't lose a deal. Be nice, never accusatory, or argumentative, to win at this game. Be willing to win some and lose some. (This technique is most appropriate for a business buyer who does not have to quickly buy a business. If you are unemployed and living on your savings, do what it takes to buy a decent business ASAP. You can play master negotiator from the safety of your cash cow, the business you buy next week.)

Regardless of your situation, you can win more with this simple technique: "Mr. Seller, I understand your position. Let me think about it and run it by my *Business Buyer Advocate*." Some owners are so motivated to sell to you that they will blurt out (then or later), "Oh, never mind. Let's do a deal."

Never forget (if you can afford to keep looking) that another good acquisition is around the corner.

Ask—don't be shy.

Ask to receive.

Don't ask and you won't get. The answer is "no" if you don't ask. Don't be afraid of making offers to sellers or to negotiate with them. Don't let your fear of being rejected stop you. This is a mistake that amateur buyers make; it keeps them on the sidelines. Don't imagine what the seller might accept. Propose, shut up, listen, and then negotiate. You will forego the chance to make or save money if you don't ask. Asking isn't as painful as you imagine; it is less painful than making a bad deal or no deal at all. Not convinced?

Read the book about how to ask effectively: *The Aladdin Factor*, by Mark Victor Hanson and Jack Canfield.

Don't rely on anyone working both sides of the street.

Avoid conflict-of-interest and bad advice. Do not rely on an advisor or intermediary that works for you and the seller. Be suspicious when someone wants you to believe their primary loyalty is to the "transaction" instead of the buyer or seller.

Use the optimum legal entity to buy and to operate.

Too many buyers use the wrong kind of legal entity as the purchaser, or the acquired company is not operated by the best kind of legal structure. If you discover this after buying: Why didn't your attorney adequately advise you? Or did you do it your way, which is exposing you to problems you could have averted?

Don't be a greater fool.

The greater fool theory is the belief by some people who make a poor investment that later they will be able to sell it at a higher price than they paid to "a greater fool."

Most businesses are not worth buying. Their owners hope for a naive buyer to take their business off their hands.

Search for the winners.

According to IRS statistics, only 1 out of 5 privately held businesses pay the owner a salary and benefits (at market rates) plus earn enough profit for the business, after the buyer's purchase of it, to pay for itself and provide a decent return on and of the buyer's investment.

This story we call "In Search of a Greater Fool." It's about a business acquisition gone bad which caused the new owner to attempt to unload the business on a greater fool. The business' buyer, who is now the seller, is a CPA who worked in the finance department of a large corporation. He bought a custom cabinet shop. He still owes about 25% on the acquisition debt. He's willing to sell the business for what he paid for it, but he suspects this will be difficult because he overpaid for the business. The only offer he's had was for 30% less than his acquisition price. Other buyers told him they weren't interested because for his asking price and down payment they could buy a larger, more profitable business. He realizes the type of business he owns will be hard to sell to another corporate refugee. The "natural" buyer for the business is someone in the trade, but most of those people don't have enough cash or borrowing power to do the deal. He claims part of his problem can be traced to the former owner having "cooked the books" and concealing important information. His lawyer says sue the seller, but he's hesitant to do so. He relies upon the former owner for advice during his transition into the business and he needs the former owner's cooperation to re-sell the company. Moreover, this CPA is afraid the former owner might not permit the assignment of his promissory note. The CPA wonders why he got into a construction related business. He doesn't understand the industry. He doesn't understand the culture, meaning the employees. "All they seem to live for are cigarette breaks and going home for a beer." He's at the end of his rope. To buy the business he had to sell stock, real estate, and exercise stock options. Most of the business' net cash flow, after debt service, has gone to pay taxes.

Moral to the story? Don't be a greater fool than the seller or competing buyers.

Don't do a dumb deal.

According to the thousands of people we've informed over the past four decades, our topic, "Anatomy of a Dumb Deal," is one of the most popular and eye-opening parts of our *Business Buyer Training*™. During it we detail *The Street-Smart Way to Buy a Business*®. Here's why:

One of the biggest contributors to a dumb deal occurs when naïve buyers erroneously adjust, recast, and normalize the financial statements of a company for sale.

In our example of a dumb deal, the six-figure annual net profit the seller touts is really a five-figure net loss for the unsuspecting buyer. The adjustments, by the seller and the seller's representatives, shown to potential buyers seem plausible (but not to people with sufficient experience achieving successful acquisitions).

Sellers are delighted by eager, uninformed competition among buyers.

Wondering about the second most memorable part of *Buyer Training*? The example we show of a liquidation scenario, which is what hapless buyers can experience if they do a dumb deal.

Don't be afraid to tell it like it is—but do it carefully.

Most owners of small and midsize businesses respect people who say what they mean and mean what they say. Unlike corporate or government life, where excessive political correctness obscures what people need to know, in small business being tactful and direct can be a good thing. Of course, you should try to avoid offending business sellers. Mirroring their style of communication, when conversing with them, can make your no-nonsense words more tolerable, and get across your points.

Don't be trumped by bluffing.

Let's focus on the buying and selling of small and midsize companies. And we'll do it in the context of the incessant news media's coverage of President Trump's "Art of the Bluff."

Here's what usually happens to naïve people who want to buy a business:

They play their bluff card when they think they are talking to a desperate seller.

Buyers: Beware the unintended consequence. If you "win" you can end of owning an unfixable loser. After all, why would the seller of a worthwhile company agree to terms that appear to totally benefit the buyer . . . unless the seller was looking for a greater fool.

There's another risk in bluffing. It happens when sellers walk away, and then they tell everyone else in their industry that wannabe buyer, so-and-so, is looking to steal a company. That can shut the buyer out of an entire industry.

Donald Trump is famous for demanding unreasonable concessions from his opponents. When it works, as he wants it to work, it may be good for him. And he can afford it when people decline his ultimatums. Can you?

Don't start with a lowball offer.

Instead of starting your negotiation with a lowball offer, keep the ball in play. Privately compute the reasonable range of value for the company you might buy. And then begin by offering terms at the low end of the range.

The seller probably won't keep talking to you unless you show written evidence for your initial offer. Sweeten the pie by telling the seller that the price could go up if, during due diligence, you can prove all the seller's claims and if you see potential growth for the company.

Later, you can adjust the price up or down as you discover more about the company and its owner.

Negotiating by a thousand cuts can be smarter than a take-it-or-leave it initial offer.

Don't unnecessarily or too early play hardball.

The closer you and the seller get to closing, the more influence you may have to get reasonable last-minute concessions from the seller. Taking unfair advantage of the seller can come back to haunt you, before and after closing.

Don't fail to negotiate but don't negotiate to failure.

The answer is "no" if you don't ask. Diplomatically communicate what you want, why you want it and why it is also in the other side's self-interest to give you what you want. But refrain from pushing too hard on everything; that is a good way to be told to take a hike.

Don't negotiate with blinders on.

Don't negotiate with blinders on. It is essential that you identify each of the goals you want to achieve by purchasing a business.

It is equally essential that you determine the goals the owner wants to achieve by selling the business. His goals might include:

- providing liquidity for investment or for his estate

- selling at the time he thinks is the top of the market

- selling at a price and terms that net him more money than he gets from owning the business

- avoiding additional investment in the business to keep up with or defeat competitors

- to comply with governmental regulations.

Don't let anyone decide for you.

Savvy buyers invest in expert advice because it is their money and peace-of-mind at risk. Don't permit friends, family, or advisors to decide for you. Finish the analysis of your goals and the seller's goals before you negotiate. If you don't, it's like shooting at a moving target—with blinders on.

Don't foul the allocation of the purchase price.

Allocation of the buy/sell price can be as important as the price itself. The parties to the transaction should agree upon the allocation of purchase price early in their negotiations. Compromises are necessary and usual. Deferring (at least a preliminary discussion of it) until escrow (i.e., moments before the intended closing) may be when the parties realize they cannot agree on a win-win allocation. This can cost all parties a considerable amount of time and money if the deal falls through.

It is essential that the parties to a buy/sell transaction can explicitly explain their economic justification for the prices (values) ascribed to each element of the allocation of consideration paid for a business, especially the valuation of acquired intangible assets.

According to Lorie Blum, CPA: "Asset classification to maximize return and lessen taxes is part science and part art. The larger the transaction the more likely there will have to be a formal valuation performed, wherein some or many of the various asset values may be indicated."

Some accountants and attorneys have not mastered the art of allocation of the purchase price, which is part of the Definitive Sale and Purchase Agreement. Adverse consequences can arise with respect to the amount of the price allocated to the seller's covenant not to compete. Some methodologies have been rejected by the courts.

In the USA, both the seller and buyer must prepare and attach IRS Form 8594, Asset Acquisition Statement, to their income tax return for the year the sale occurred.

Understand the effect of down payment on price.

According to Toby Tatum's book, *Transaction Patterns*: Acquisitions that were financed by the seller sold for a 15% (median) higher price than all-cash transactions. The average down payment was 37%. "This difference is more pronounced if we compare the all-cash transaction to those selling with seller financing of 70% or more." In these deals, the median sale price was 27% higher than all-cash transactions.

Don't use all your money for the down payment.

Don't use all your liquid funds for the down payment. Reserve cash to pay advisors, closing costs and for working capital (which you might have to deposit into the company shortly after you purchase it). It's also a good idea to have cash in an emergency reserve.

Don't outbid ignorant buyers.

Corporate downsizing creates a horde of unemployed, inexperienced business buyers. They congregate around advertised and broker-listed businesses because these are the companies easiest to find. Few of these people know how to buy a company. They are a major threat to you because they naively bid-up the price and down payment. They create a sellers' market.

Don't let disruptive innovations surprise you.

Don't let industry-wide disruptive innovations leave your company in the dust. Disruptive innovation, sudden and overwhelming, frequently by upstarts, attacks established industries. It is going from the way it was to how it is going to be.

Opportunities to benefit from disruption exist for longstanding players if they anticipate what is coming and then join the leading edge of progress. Think about it: Few so-called disruptive initiatives, which upset the established marketplace, emerge out of nowhere. Usually word leaks out; people talk; market testing hints at what's coming. That's the time for established companies to get on the band wagon.

According to freelance writer, Estel Masangkay, on *Wired Innovation Insights*, "disruptive innovations use alternative technologies to offer consumers a better/cheaper mousetrap. Innovations are often disguised as 'alternatives' and 'options' to established technologies. Potential disruptive innovations often pass under the radar with their unassuming appearance, but don't be fooled. Disruption may be hard to spot under their disguises, but they have the capacity to change the game and remake the rules."

An example is the digital revolution, in the form of Uber, Lyft and other ride-sharing companies, which is devastating the taxi industry. Imagine the plight of the buyers of taxi medallions who didn't see the writing on the wall. Another example is Airbnb, the controversial (disruptive) online marketplace that lets people rent out rooms in their homes—competing with hotels. How about the product delivery business? Amazon and Target are looking into the delivery of goods by drone. What about the iPod, iPad, and iPhone?

What stops incumbent companies from adopting the disruptive innovation? Except, perhaps, in the obvious case of Apple, the early customers of disruptive technology are a relatively smaller and less profitable market than the purchasers of products sold by the incumbent companies. Industry startups, in contrast, don't have anything to sell but their innovation, and with nothing to defend or retool they can direct all their resources to exploit the opportunity.

Some far-seeing companies use mergers and acquisitions to acquire new, emerging business models. For some, doing that is easier, faster, and more profitable to keep up with marketplace changes and to grow the company than trying to extend the company's resources (talent and money) to get on the band wagon.

Don't overlook demographic changes in the workforce.

Are you and the company you want to acquire prepared for demographic changes in the workforce?

The Society for Human Resource Management, "2014 Older Workers Survey," found that one-third of organizations fear that the potential loss of older-worker talent could be a problem for their industry or organization. One in five said their organizations had no strategies to transfer knowledge from older to younger workers. Business buyers who don't investigate and plan for this before acquiring companies will have to cope with the potential adverse effects during their ownership.

Don't feel secure without employment contracts.

You and your company will have more peace-of-mind and be more secure if key staff members sign an employment contract. Ask the owner and key employees before acquiring a business. Ask employees afterwards, if you bought a company whose key employees didn't commit before closing, to remain employed for a reasonable amount of time post-acquisition.

Carefully negotiate contractual default provisions.

This is where savvy legal counsel is necessary.

Here's an example of what can go wrong if your purchase and sale agreement is deficient with respect to this scenario: You can lose your investment in the business if your purchase agreement and security agreement, which you pledge to the seller for partially financing your purchase, provides for you to lose your rights to the business if you fail to make even one installment payment on your promissory note to the seller.

Don't agree to an unreasonable acceleration clause in promissory notes.

Don't miscalculate your business buying risk.

Elements of potential loss include: Amount by which you might overpay, your down payment, personal guarantees, acquisition debt, professional fees, commission to seller's business broker, lost income while searching for businesses, business losses, capital you add to support the business, and other surprises caused by poor due diligence. What would be the adverse effect on your time, health, marriage, self-esteem, employment, and credit rating if the business fails or if you cannot sell it for what you paid?

Culture incompatibilities can stymie you.

McKinsey & Company refers to a company's cultural environment as "the way we do things around here." Most of the time what we read about cultural incompatibilities is in relation to M&A transactions where there is too much friction during the integration of two or more companies.

It is reported that up to half of mergers fail due to incompatibilities. Irreconcilable differences can arise, for example, when a white-collar purchaser acquires a blue-collar company or vice versa. Or when a micro-manager acquires a business formerly run by a big-picture owner who was comfortable delegating to others. Or where the new owner is a ditherer compared to the fast-deciding former owner.

Don't assume the employee mix must continue.

Sometimes a business can become more successful if certain kinds of fulltime employees are replaced with part-timers or with outsourced labor.

Don't create a negotiating free-fall.

There will be numerous controversies to negotiate. Do not state your position on any of them until you have heard all the issues for which someone (seller, broker, landlord, etc.) seeks a concession from you. You might say, "George, why don't you make a list of everything you want from me, and then explain and justify what you want? That way we can quickly get through the process for a win-win deal." Of course, you won't ever make such a list for the other side of a negotiation. Whoever creates the first list is at a disadvantage. Once you know the scope of the issues and the relative materiality among them, you can devise a master strategy to negotiate. Know the big picture before you tackle the details. First discuss and reach agreement on the easiest, least contentious issues. You won't get everything you want, but you will be better off than had you coped with each item as it arose.

Find the bridge to seller agreement.

Reconciling buyer and seller perspective on valuation is necessary, especially when the parties are far apart.

Start with common sense. The value of a company to its owner is different from its value to a business purchaser. The owner bases his opinion of value upon what he *knows* about the company's future. Buyers cannot know as much as sellers, so they offset their risk by lowering the seller's value. Some buyers, however, see a better future than the seller, because of what the buyer intends to do with the company. This can increase the price the buyer is willing to pay.

A reasonable value for a business, to an owner who is not selling, is the present value of a (reasonably) certain stream of future income. The strategic decision an owner makes is: What alternatives to my business exist for the investment of money and talent that I dedicate to my business?

Don't permit the deal to be over when it shouldn't be.

If, after closing, you discover facts detrimental that the seller did not disclose to you, shouldn't you have effective recourse against the seller? Ask your attorney how to provide for this.

Don't overcomplicate the deal.

Unless you are involved in a high-value M&A transaction or are trying to buy a high-risk business, refrain from overcomplicating your nonbinding letter of intent, due diligence, dealmaking and the contract of purchase.

Don't err with advisors.

Accountants and lawyers can help you make a better deal, which includes the protection of your downside. You can err with accountants and lawyers by not employing them to help you buy a business. You can also err by giving them unlimited scope. These advisors have a technical role (contracts, legal exposure, and the implications of financial statements). Be careful using them for business acquisition go/no-go advice.

Don't waste money on advisors.

You can minimize the fees you pay for professional services. These fees can take your breath way if you don't control them.

Do your homework about the business before you make assignments to experts, so you can save time and money and get better results from them.

- Ask your lawyer what is the worst thing that can happen, and how you can mitigate your risk and still do the deal?

- Ask your accountant and business consultant the same thing.

- Ask your accountant and business appraiser for a list of additional information you should review.

- Ask your appraiser to value the business based upon what is and what would be if you achieve profit targets you set for your acquisition.

Early in your due diligence, get a *Ballpark Price Fairness Opinion* from an independent, credible appraiser. Use this to test the seller's asking price and your opinion of value against marketplace reality. This tip will only cost you a few hundred dollars. It may save you countless weeks or months trying to do a deal with a seller who will not accept reality. It's how street-smart business buyers test the water with respect to the seller's asking price.

Don't cut out brokers.

There can be serious legal penalties if you are involved in an attempt to cheat a broker out of the broker's sales commission. If a business broker hired by the seller is the procuring cause for you discovering a business for sale, or if you directly approach a company and later find out it is represented by a broker, do not suggest or conspire with the seller to cut out the broker.

Procuring cause is widely interpreted and may be defined in the listing agreement between the broker and seller. Encompassed in the definition could be the simple fact that a broker tells you he has a listing for the business, shows you information about it and/or introduces you to the owner. Courts have ruled that the buyer had to pay the broker's commission, treble damages, and attorney's fees where it was proven the buyer concealed a purchase from the broker because of the buyer's unfair and deceptive practices.

Avoid charges of bad faith, deception, conspiracy, and tortuous interference in contractual relationships, among others. Don't try to slip your surrogate in to purchase the business during or after the expiration of the broker listing. Play fairly.

Don't sign a purchase offer before legal counsel sees it.

Your attorney's job is to protect your legal interest, especially your downside. Use your *Business Buyer Advocate* to help you assess your business interests.

Don't overlook contingencies for the buy/sell contract.

The purchase price should be subject to confirmation by an independent business appraisal firm employed and paid by the buyer at the conclusion of the buyer's investigation of the business. There should be adequate time to examine detailed books and records; transfer leases/titles/ownership; adjust inventory; repair/replace defective assets at seller's expense; interview key employees, customers, suppliers; complete buyer's period of onsite observation of the business prior to closing; comply with governmental regulations; disclose off-balance sheet items and contingent liabilities; pay liabilities. Your attorney will suggest other items.

Don't be the bearer of bad news.

Rely on your acquisition advisor to wear the black hat so you avoid arguments with the seller, broker, and others. Use a third party to provide a credible business valuation so you can avoid losing the deal because of a price argument between you and the seller. An independent valuation can convince the seller's advisors that your offer is fair.

Don't surprise sellers and brokers.

Be nice. Avoid misunderstandings, delays, and aborted deals. Tell sellers and brokers upfront exactly what you expect from them.

Don't waive recourse against brokers or sellers.

Waiving recourse is a good way to wave goodbye to your money and peace-of-mind.

Myths about the broker's commission.

"The seller pays the business broker's sales commission—the buyer doesn't." The down payment and the price include the commission. The seller pays the commission from *your* money. Buyers usually need less cash and borrowing power when the seller does not have to pay a commission.

Let's do the math. Assume a business purchase price is $500,000, the down payment is 50% and the broker's commission is 10%. Your $250,000 down payment is reduced by the $50,000 broker commission. The seller nets $200,000.

However, if you bought the business without a broker's representation of the seller, your down payment could be $50,000 less and the seller would still net $200,000. What else could you do with $50,000, which you don't need for the down payment? Or, if you want to make a $250,000 down payment, how much of a discount from the price would the seller concede?

Don't underestimate the importance of what you may think is a mere $50,000, especially when you realize we're talking about after-tax dollars. Think what you can buy with $50,000 (toys, fun, and education). $50,000 is not small change to most people. $50,000 can make the difference between a deal that closes and one that doesn't.

Okay, in the spirit of fair and balanced, here's a broker's response to what I write above:

"I get a kick out of this. It is the same language in the *Real Estate for Sale by Owner Magazine* wherein home sellers advertise their property for sale. The enticement is that somehow buyers and sellers can save the broker's fee. That is the real myth. According to studies conducted by the Texas A & M University's real estate department, buyers who bought from a FSBO paid 30% more on average for homes than those who used a broker. I believe that is similar in business sales. Frankly, it takes a broker to get a reasonable price for a business. Buyers will offer less when they know there is no broker, so who saves the commission. No one. Brokers educate the sellers regarding the value of their businesses. Most sellers have no idea as to value. Often their idea of value is the amount of money they need to retire for the next 20 years. Here is another fact, less than 30% of all the businesses for sale ever actually sell. They just go out of business when the owner can no longer operate the business or when the owner has something else he wants to do."

The most important point the broker makes, above, is buyers with effective representation do better than do-it-yourselfers.

Don't negotiate on the fly.

Define negotiating strategy in advance so you know what to expect from the seller and how to react.

Don't be a smarty-pants.

Don't get sucked into the trap: "What do *you* think?" When the seller or broker wants your opinion about the asking price, say this:

"It would be presumptuous of me to disagree with the seller on price or terms because I don't know everything the seller knows upon which he bases his asking terms." Do NOT challenge the seller's price or terms until the seller completes the due diligence question-naires you provide to him. You do not know enough to have an informed opinion. Sellers are precious. Romance them; don't dump them too soon.

Don't settle for the seller's reason for sale.

Don't settle for the seller's reason for sale. It might be *one* of the legitimate reasons why he wants to sell his business. Every now and then, repeat the question; phrase it so it does not sound repetitive. And then later when you interview people about the business, ask them why they think the owner wants to sell. (Get the owner's writ-ten permission to divulge the potential sale of the business.)

Define the "price."

What, exactly, do you get for the price you pay? Example: Corporate shares, tangible and intangible assets, known and un-known liabilities. How about the assumption or assignment of leases, lines of credit or the ownership interest in another busi-ness? Do you get the business' website, telephone number, Yellow Pages listing and email address? Who owns the business name (and trademarks, patents, etc.)? What about the customer and supplier lists? What about the list of prospective customers and people who made inquiries? Do you get policy and procedure manuals and an employee handbook that defines all the job descriptions? Are there grandfather clauses in contracts or governmental regulations that will or will not survive the sale of the business? What about the seller's covenant not to compete and/or agreement to consult with you or continue as an employee?

Bottom line: Acquire the assets that are reasonably and ordinarily necessary to operate the business. Decline or put a leash on liabilities.

Don't disregard this negotiating tip.

Sometimes during due diligence and negotiations you will be at an impasse; you and the seller cannot agree. Fighting about the controversial issue will kill the pending transaction. When this occurs, you can say: "Mr. Seller, let's not try to handle this now. Instead, let's work on other issues, okay?"

You can afford to do this because you are following our advice, which is to always have more than one potential acquisition in due diligence. Later, you might abandon this company for a better one or you might not have an objection because you found enough benefits in the business to cause you to stop fighting.

Don't be too eager or standoffish.

Showing your emotions and being too specific about your motive to buy a business may cause the seller and broker to raise the price or to demand terms that favor the seller. On the other hand, if you are too aloof the seller might seek other buyers.

Don't let emotion triumph logic.

Controversy, misunderstanding, and disagreement are normal during dealmaking. Don't get so angry that you or the seller aborts your transaction in the face of common sense that says the deal is worth doing, despite your personalities.

Don't buy a business as-is.

You might buy real estate as-is, but don't do it when you buy a business. The seller should provide various representations and warranties and then indemnify you for them, all of which is stipulated in your purchase contract. It might also be wise for the seller to pledge security to you if too big an unknown exists. One technique is a reserve which the seller funds with enough cash or other assets for a specified time after closing against which you can draw if undisclosed liabilities or excessive A/R bad debts occur.

Jane Musgrave, staff writer for the *Palm Beach Post*, in her article, "Hold maker of dust spray accountable, lawsuit says," writes: Limping into court a man asked a judge to allow him to seek hundreds of thousands, if not millions, of dollars from companies that sold a young woman a potent chemical that she sucked down before involving him in an automobile crash, which occurred several years ago. The case, if it succeeds, would be among the first in the nation to hold the makers of computer dusters responsible for injuries caused by what is known as huffing. The attorney representing the injured party said companies can be held responsible for ignoring evidence that their product is being misused.

Spot the opportunities for negotiation.

Buyers want recourse after their purchase if they discover that assets are worth less than represented or liabilities are more than the seller stated. Buyers document the seller's representations and warranties in the buy/sell contract, which imposes penalties when facts are not as the seller promises or infers. It's normal for sellers to resist (at the behest of their attorney). They want the deal to be over at closing. Their reluctance can be a deal killer, or it can be your opportunity to negotiate. You and the seller can resolve your dilemma if you cooperate in good faith and effectively communicate.

Brian Baldwin, a specialist in private investment banking with Baldwin & Associates, Bellevue WA, offers these tips. Consider using the phrase, "to the best of the seller's knowledge," as a qualifier. You might be willing to accept that some amount of breaching of representations and warranties is unavoidable, in which case you are willing to accept a dollar limit up to which the seller will not be held responsible. Perhaps putting a time limit on the duration of some of the representations and warranties will facilitate a deal. Maybe the seller will provide the representation and warranty in return for a higher sale price (and vice versa). It's common for buyers and sellers to use a combination of these ideas to make a deal.

You might have to give—to get seller warranties.

Don't expect the seller to give you all the contractual warranties you want without your reciprocation. Typical sellers warrant the usefulness of the company's assets and they warrant the truthfulness of other important facts about the company. The seller's breach of such warranties might compensate you or otherwise provide relief for what will occur if what you bought is not consistent with what the seller represented to be what was sold to you.

In return for these assurances and guarantees, smart sellers (especially sellers that partially finance your purchase) may include language in the sale and purchase agreement that commits you to properly manage the assets and liabilities of the business. There are other expectations that your attorney can explain to you.

Don't leave deposits unspoken for.

During due diligence you will probably discover various deposits that the company has made regarding leases, suppliers, public utilities, and retainers held by professional advisors. Who gets these deposits?

Don't overlook any kind of tax collector.

Some states and localities impose transfer taxes. Before you make the deal, find out if this applies, especially if real estate is part of your acquisition.

Budget for yourself a realistic management salary.

Don't set an unrealistically high or low compensation package for yourself as the new owner. Sources of financing frown upon buyers who overpay themselves. The business can pay you more than it paid the former owner if you increase the business' profit and if your compensation does not violate your agreement with the seller and/or sources of financing.

You don't have to take a cut in pay if you buy right.

Think twice before buying a business that does not have the capacity for your first-year salary to be no less than your former pay.

Why accept a cut in pay? Buy the right business the right way to immediately earn a management salary no less than your most recent salary. But that is not enough. Additionally, the company should earn enough profit (exclusive of your compensation), from day one, to satisfy your target return on investment and have the capability for you to recoup your initial investment (down payment and perhaps the cash you put into the business for working capital shortly after buying it) over the first few years.

Of course, leaving positive cash flow in the business makes sense if it can be used to make more money.

Don't ignore ROI.

It's important not to pay more than a business is worth. It's more important to know, before you make an offer to purchase, if the business will achieve your target return on investment.

Don't be overly wowed by positive cash flow.

It is easy to tout positive cash flow to conceal net loss. Here's an explanation provided by an expert.

Harold Averkamp, CPA, MBA, AccountingCoach.com:

How can a company with a net loss show a positive cash flow?

A common explanation for a company with a net loss to report a positive cash flow is depreciation expense. Depreciation expense reduces a company's net income (or increases its net loss), but it does not involve a payment of cash in the current period. For example, if a company purchased equipment last year for $2,100,000 and depreciates the equipment over seven years, its depreciation expense this year might be $300,000. This year's $300,000 entry involves a debit to Depreciation Expense and a credit to Accumulated Depreciation. Not a penny left the checking account this year. (All $2,100,000 of cash left the checking account last year.) If the company's income statement reports a loss of $50,000 after the $300,000 "non-cash" depreciation expense, its cash may have increased by $250,000.

Another explanation involves accrual accounting. A corporation must report its expenses as they are incurred and that is often before the corporation pays the invoice. For example, a corporation with an accounting year ending December 31 might have a huge expense at the end of 2012, but the invoice is not due until January 2013. The 2012 net income was reduced, but the corporation's cash is not reduced until 2013.

Here's another example. A corporation might receive a deposit from one of its customers in December 2012 but will not earn the revenues until 2013. In that case, the corporation's cash increased in 2012, but the corporation's revenues and net income will not increase until 2013.

It is a good idea to get comfortable reading the statement of cash flows. It should be included with a corporation's income statement and balance sheet.

Don't forget post-acquisition after-tax cash flow.

Forecast after-tax cash flow.

If payments on acquisition debt exceed 50% of net profit, trade credit is harder to get, and your risk of insolvency grows. Buyers who do not realize the *principal* portion of payments is paid in *after-tax* dollars risk a cash flow crisis.

Insulting the seller is unwise.

The seller probably did homework to arrive at his asking price. You, too, should get expert advice before you make your initial offer to purchase. There are few businesses for sale that fully match your acquisition criteria. Don't be thrown out of the seller's office because you make a ridiculous offer. Do not be rigid or aloof. Be flexible.

Speed bumps don't have to block opportunity.

When you and the seller are getting too far apart, and you and/or the seller are about to abort your deal, make a list of points on which you both agree. Make a list of what you cannot (so far) agree upon. Make a list of factors that remain open to negotiation. Are you sure you should not continue your pursuit of the business?

Ask your *Business Buyer Advocate* to mediate. It's like marriage counseling. Don't let the inability of you and the seller to communicate block what could be a good thing. Getting your way is not as important as making a reasonable investment in a business that can provide the lifestyle and income you desire.

Don't misadjust inventory at closing.

At escrow, if inventory is less than the seller originally represented, adjust the price and the *down payment* (otherwise, you will spend cash, post-acquisition, to increase the inventory to the represented level). If inventory at closing exceeds the originally represented amount, the adjustment should be to the price and the *promissory note* (not down payment).

Don't lie.

If you don't have the financial or managerial capability to buy and successfully manage the business, change your acquisition criteria. Search for businesses that fit you.

Don't be a smart aleck.

It's taken for granted that you are smart and capable. Don't aggravate brokers, sellers, landlords or anyone else to show them how smart you are or that they should not fool with you. Some of the best trial lawyers politely peel the skin off their adversaries.

Ask questions; don't lecture.

Spend less time trying to show the seller how smart you are and devote more time to asking questions and getting complete answers to every question. Refrain from voicing your opinion about the answers until you've asked all your questions and after you have reviewed all the answers with your acquisition team.

Don't accept the owner at face value.

The seller wears his war face when he talks to you. The purpose of what he says to you is to influence you in his favor. Look beyond the business and the seller's personal story. Do a thorough background check on him. You might discover the real reason why the business is for sale, among other useful facts.

Don't buy too fast.

Anxiety can kill. Patience can pay. There are numerous good reasons to delay buying a business. Don't put yourself in a position where you might have to quickly sell the business shortly after buying it. First clean up messes in your personal (medical, divorce) and financial life. It is risky to buy a business if you have recently moved to an unfamiliar region, or if you want to buy a company that is outside your business experience (i.e., you're from manufacturing but you want to own a retailer).

From a *Wall Street Journal* article, "Buying a small company also takes patience," Jeff Bailey: An inefficient market, secretive sellers, a host of junk makes it a maze. Indeed, the market for buying and selling smaller companies is treacherously inefficient, lacking a single source for listings and any authoritative guide to what a business is worth. What's more, many sellers are overly secretive and unrealistic about the value of their business. And, plainly stated, there is a lot of junk for sale. That means that buyers who take the time to carefully investigate a purchase—the prospects of the industry, financing options, the results and reputation of the individual company—stand a better chance of success than those who wing it.

Don't disclose all your assets to sellers or brokers.

Doing so will cause them to want more from you. Only show enough of your financial capability to demonstrate your ability to make the purchase.

Don't kiss and tell.

Do not divulge to anyone (except your business acquisition advisors) that a particular company is for sale or anything about the business. It's not ethical. Moreover, if you buy a business in an industry in which you have interviewed several sellers, and then revealed their confidential info, these business owners will not be pleasant competitors when it comes to you.

Don't believe promises.

Get it in writing (preferably contractual before you buy the business) when a seller, key employee, large customer, essential supplier, or source of financing says you can count on them for anything that is substantially important to the company you might acquire.

Don't prematurely discuss price and terms.

Never discuss price and terms with sellers or business brokers before you have examined the business' financial statements and interviewed the seller on the nonfinancial factors that influence value. It would be presumptuous of you to state an opinion about the business' value before this. Doing so could prevent you from making a good acquisition.

Don't accept the asking price.

Ask the seller to explain the rationale for the asking price. If his initial explanation does not make sense, it probably won't get any better. If his rationale is reasonable, do not argue about it. Proceed with due diligence.

Don't be first to propose deal structure.

You can avoid negotiating with yourself by asking the seller to describe the structure of the contemplated transaction, and the seller's rationale for it, before you tell the seller how you would like to structure the terms of sale and purchase.

Consider starting with a letter of intent (LOI).

What about a Letter of Intent (nonbinding)?

Too many principals (and advisors) to buy/sell transactions do not adequately understand the purpose of, the optimum timing of and the content of a letter of intent.

With an executed letter of intent in hand, the buyer and seller may be more willing to commit additional resources toward the achievement of a done deal.

Letters of intent can be deal killers unless the buyer and seller agree on the content thereof; compromises are necessary and usual.

The article, "Letters of Intent—a Trap for the Unwary," by attorneys Thomas C. Homburger and James R. Schueller, shows how a "nonbinding" letter of intent can be a trap. A poorly drafted letter of intent may impose obligations and liabilities that the parties to it did not intend. Some courts have held that a buyer and seller who execute an otherwise nonbinding letter of intent have a duty of good faith to negotiate a definitive agreement with the other party. Moreover, a nonbinding letter of intent may in fact be construed to be binding depending upon the terms (or the absence of essential terms) of the agreement.

According to an American Bar Association publication, *Letter of Intent*: "A letter of intent is often entered into between a buyer and a seller following the successful completion of the first phase of negotiations of an acquisition transaction. The letter generally, but not always, describes the purchase price (or a formula for determining the purchase price) and certain other key economic and procedural terms that form the basis for further negotiations. In most cases, the buyer and the seller do not yet intend to be legally bound to consummate the transaction and expect that the letter of intent will be superseded by a definitive written acquisition agreement. Alternatively, buyers and sellers may prefer a memorandum of understanding or a term sheet to reflect deal terms. Although the seller and the buyer will generally desire the substantive deal terms outlined in a letter of intent to be nonbinding expressions of their then current understanding of the shape of the prospective transaction, letters of intent frequently contain some provisions that the parties intend to be binding."

Starting with a purchase contract may not be wise.

Think about whether a nonbinding letter of intent should precede the purchase offer and contract. You could use an LOI to test the water with the seller. If you can't reach agreement on the terms of a nonbinding letter of intent (it is inexpensive to draft), you won't waste thousands of dollars in legal fees for your attorney to prepare a definitive contract.

Don't accept pitfalls in the purchase contract.

To neutralize pitfalls, amend dangerous clauses in purchase contracts presented by sellers and brokers.

Remember to protect your confidentiality.

If you don't want everyone, including competitors to the company you buy, to know the details of whatever you disclosed to the seller or the terms of your purchase agreement with the seller, the definitive agreement (or other contract) should prohibit the seller from disclosing your information. If a business broker was involved, get a non-disclosure document from him, too.

Don't ask anyone to breach their confidentiality or noncompetition agreement with their present or previous employer or any other relationship. Find ethical ways to discover what you need to know about a company, its competition, its industry, and its owners.

Don't buy on a gentlemen's agreement.

If it's not in the definitive agreement, it becomes he-said, she-said. In other words, you don't have a leg to stand on. Reject sellers who pooh-pooh your concern about lack of documentation. "Don't worry, you have my word. We have a gentleman's agreement."

Don't settle for less than definitive.

Your definitive agreement should be definitive. It should contain all pertinent information relating to the acquisition, sale, or merger, including but not limited to the agreed price, the financing of the business and the timing for closing the transaction. Include details about what the purchase or merger includes and excludes such as specific assets and liabilities. Plus, representations and warranties, covenants, conditions, indemnification, termination procedures and remedies. Related documents could include non-compete, employment and consulting agreements, assignment of leases, financing documents, etc.

Don't give the seller free hand to manage the company.

Don't give the seller a free hand to manage the business. As soon as it is certain that you and the seller will do a deal, reach agreement with the seller about what he can and cannot do between then and closing (and the seller's behavior as you transition into the company). The last thing you need is for the seller to obligate the business for something you don't want.

Don't imagine what the seller thinks.

Don't lose a deal because you are wrong about the seller's position. Ask him to tell you exactly why he believes what he says to you.

You don't have to lose a deal because of price.

Don't lose a deal on a good company because of price. An axiom says: You set the price and I set the terms of purchase.

You might agree to pay a price that is acceptable to the seller but is not acceptable to you—if you get favorable purchase terms, such as seller financing or an earnout.

An earnout refers to an additional payment in a merger or acquisition, which is not part of the original acquisition price; it is based on the acquired company's future earnings relative to a baseline amount determined in the buy/sell agreement. An earnout is a price contingency. The typical earnout divides the purchase consideration between payment at closing and one or more contingent payments dependent upon the satisfaction of future revenue targets, product developments, earnings, or other milestones. An earnout is appropriate when used to acquire a young company or one on the verge of extraordinary success (or risk), where the buyer (and maybe the seller) is not sure of the certainty of the profit forecast.

You don't have to, upfront, buy the entire company.

Maybe your best strategy is to buy part of the company, with an option to later purchase the rest upon agreed terms. Or use an option to buy and then take a management (or other important) role in the company.

Don't neglect tax implications.

How you structure the purchase has a material effect on taxation for you and the seller. Consider the purchase document, allocation of the elements of purchase, installment sale, royalty or earnout, profit sharing, bartering, seller's agreement not to compete, employment/consulting contracts, etc.

Don't blindly assume contracts.

Examine each contract. If you would not have signed it had you been the owner, maybe you should not accept it now. Try to get a concession from the seller to mitigate your risk; alternatively, you and/or the seller can try to renegotiate the agreement that bothers you.

Check landlord's reputation early during your review.

Investigate the landlord's character and business practices. If a property manager is involved, investigate that person and firm also. Besides checking references, check the courts for a history of litigation by individuals and businesses.

Be alert to cases where the landlord is in default under the terms of leases with tenants, especially within the building or complex you will occupy; this can affect your cost of leasing and it can affect how the property is managed during your tenancy.

Before you contact a landlord, attorney, or leasing agent, get strategic advice from a business consultant. This impartial person is necessary to quarterback your use of other advisors—to make sure you know the right questions to ask and get appropriate answers.

Always take a proposed lease to an attorney who specializes in commercial leases.

It is also smart to get an opinion from a commercial leasing agent, even if you must pay a nominal fee for the review. One way to avoid paying a leasing agent a consulting fee is to ask the agent to represent you. The agent won't charge you for his service. The building owner pays a commission to the agent for bringing a tenant to the negotiating table. A good agent can obtain concessions from building owners that are not available to most people who attempt to lease space directly from an owner.

Don't waste time because of uncooperative landlords.

Don't invest too much time on a potential business acquisition if the landlord is not willing to permit the assignment of the lease.

Most commercial leases require the tenant to get the landlord's permission to assign the lease. Confer with the seller early in due diligence about this and try to get the landlord to agree to an assignment. This is treacherous territory because some landlords play hardball if they believe the business is not marketable to a buyer without the landlord's cooperation. Seek legal advice because confidentiality is important; you and the seller probably do not want word to prematurely get out that the company may change hands.

Don't wait too long to commit to the landlord.

There are numerous ways that a landlord can milk the seller and the buyer in connection to the assignment of the lease to the buyer. As soon as you and the seller know you are going to consummate the transaction, execute whatever legal documents are necessary to secure the business' lease.

Don't accept a short fuse lease.

The term of the lease must be at least as long as the amount of time it will take the business to pay for itself. Add time for you to continue its operation or sell it. If the landlord won't play ball, adjust the purchase price of the business. If the seller won't play ball, pick up your glove and bat and then find another game.

Inspect the premises that come with the company.

Before you sign a new lease/sublease, obtain a recent physical inspection report which states that the property does not have defects that will cost you money for repairs in the first months of your tenancy.

Ask your lessor to certify these items are free from all defects including "latent" defects or malfunctions such as: Structural, roof, electrical/plumbing, heating/ventilation/air conditioning and toxic/environmental/ADA issues. There are more elements to check but these are vital.

Warning

Beware of any property offered to you in "as is" condition.

Don't defer too long committing to the lender(s).

There are numerous ways that sources of financing can milk the seller and the buyer in connection to the assignment or assumption of financial obligations. As soon as you and the seller know you are going to consummate the transaction, execute whatever legal documents are necessary to secure these obligations. It's a bad day for a business buyer if the bank calls or restricts the line of credit.

Don't merely eyeball the assets.

The seller should provide you with a written list / description of every tangible and intangible asset that will be conveyed to you at closing. If it's not on the list, don't expect it to be there your first day on the job.

Don't expect assets to work.

Just because you see a piece of equipment does not mean that it will properly function. Test equipment of material value. That inexpensive (but difficult to repair or replace) packaging machine at the end of the production line that does not work the day you take control means you can't ship orders to customers. Likewise, check for obsolete equipment or machinery. Review the history of equipment downtime. When and how was the repair or update handled? Who did the work, an employee, or a vendor? Anticipate downtime in your business plan.

Verify that the seller has good title to assets.

Many a business buyer has moaned upon discovering that assets in-place during his inspection were leased or on consignment—not owned by the business. Does the business use vehicles, equipment, or other assets it does not own, lease or rent? Don't assume the company owns the assets you see. Verify that the firm has unencumbered title to its assets. Tangibles, such as vehicles, furnishings and equipment and intangibles, such as trademarks, patents, and copyrights. Related, carefully assess the terms of all leases.

Don't buy without protection if there is a sole supplier.

If the business relies on a sole supplier for its equipment, machinery, or inventory—or to market and/or service its products—be careful. Your purchase contract should provide for your protection if shortly after you buy the business the sole provider is no longer available to your business and you cannot replace it without losing money.

Here's an example from a February 2015 *New York Times* story: Essential products are in short supply across the United States, an example of the widening and sometimes unexpected fallout from the gridlock at seaports on the West Coast. The impasse, caused by a protracted labor dispute between the longshoremen's union and ship owners, has brought crippling delays to sea freight in and out of the country and is wreaking havoc for retailers, food companies, farmers, and manufacturers.

Don't take too long to recoup your down payment.

Try to structure your purchase so your down payment will be recouped within three years.

The transactions I've seen during my forty-year dealmaking career put the range of the typical buyer's down payment at 20% to 40%, excluding deals with SBA financing.

Most of my clients wanted to maximize their return on investment. Leverage is one way to do so, which means minimum down payment. They also wanted to recoup their down payment as quickly as reasonably possible.

At the time of this writing, one of the requirements for an SBA business acquisition loan is a minimum 10% down payment. Most of the business brokers we know say otherwise *financially qualified buyers* should expect to make at least a 20% down payment PLUS have adequate working capital to immediately invest in the acquisition.

Nolo, the legal information website, writes: "The more common form of structuring payments in a business purchase is for you to make a down payment of perhaps 20% or 25% and then sign a promissory note agreeing to pay the balance to the seller over a number of years, in regular installments. Although down payments are usually made in cash, some buyers have been known to substitute an asset or services for all or part of the down payment."

What about no money down? The get-rich-quick promoters pitch it, but it is rarely possible for the purchase of a mature, profitable small or midsize business, which is not about to fall off a cliff. Save your money for a reasonable down payment instead of wasting it on no money down pundits.

My creative financing book explains 500 proven ways to get cash for a business you own or want to buy. Business brokers, buyers and sellers say the ideas in the book enabled them to close the purchase/sale of a business or franchise, which would not have occurred, if not for: *How to Get ALL the Money You Want For Your Business Without Stealing It* ™

Business owners/managers use some of the 200 business operation tactics to generate fast cash and improve their business.

Don't deplete your cash reserve.

One of the first facts that street-smart buyers uncover, early in their screening of companies for sale, is how much working capital is necessary. It takes more working capital if inventory is too low or if there is or will be insufficient borrowing power in the company they might acquire. Undercapitalization can put you out of business faster than operating losses.

Rarely do small and midsize businesses have sufficient cash, positive cash flow or borrowing power to seize the opportunities and to fix the problems that arise shortly after the company changes hands. It won't be good if you cannot dip into your own pocket for funding.

Keep cash and borrowing power in reserve. You may need it after you buy the business to solve a problem or exploit an opportunity. You will need to inject cash into the business shortly after you buy it for working capital.

McDonald's provides an example: Franchisees in Europe got hit hard because of the beef shortages due to mad cow disease.

Don't let others extort you.

The time to negotiate the business' relationship with its key employees and suppliers is before you buy the business. Make this a condition of closing.

Don't refrain from using your escape clause.

A good purchase contract contains reasonable escape clauses to protect the buyer. Use them to get out of a pending deal. You can go back to the seller and try to renegotiate the deal if you still want to buy the company.

You might not be able to back out.

Don't assume you can back out of a deal or renegotiate it. Savvy sellers and lawyers can force you to perform per the purchase contract, which means you might get less than what you bargained for.

Don't give the seller your blank check.

Ask your attorney about how a liquidated damages clause can protect you if you do not perform your obligations pursuant to the purchase contract. Your financial liability can exceed the amount of your earnest money deposit.

Nail down all the intangibles.

What if your purchase contract does not specify that you get the telephone numbers for the business? What other intangibles should you look for?

Your desperation doesn't have to rule you.

Don't buy because you are desperate to do "something." Lack of focus is common among unemployed people; it can suspend common sense and distort reality. If the only businesses for sale that you can find are mediocre or don't have the profit you seek, it's easy (and wrong) to think that is normal. It's not. There are numerous businesses quietly for sale on the hidden market that match your acquisition criteria.

Include "right of offset" in your purchase agreement.

Ask your attorney to include a "right of offset" in your purchase contract. This can handle misunderstandings and undisclosed liabilities that become known to you after the business changes hands. The right of offset can be used to adjust the price and payments (i.e., seller financing) due on the business purchase by crediting the cost of items such as undisclosed paid time off (vacation, sick days), unusable inventory or equipment, etc.

Don't overlook a holdback of funds contract provision.

This is another task for your attorney; it is similar to providing the buyer with the right of offset mentioned above. In this case the buyer does not want the entire purchase price conveyed to the seller, especially some or all the buyer's down payment, which is held in escrow pending transfer to the seller, until certain events transpire as agreed in the purchase and sale agreement. Among the common events that may occur after closing: Retention of key employees or customers for a certain amount of time; collection of accounts receivable; disposition of pending or threatened litigation; warranty claims by customers, etc.

The comma that cratered a deal and risked $2 million.

This excerpt from a Canadian news story, from and a long time ago, is pertinent everywhere and forever. It demonstrates the importance of careful writing and more careful proof reading.

Grant Robertson, "A basic rule of punctuation," *Globe and Mail*, 8/7/06.

It could be the costliest piece of punctuation in Canada. A grammatical blunder may force Rogers Communications Inc. to pay an extra $2.13 million to use utility poles in the Maritimes after the placement of a comma in a contract permitted the deal's cancellation. The controversial comma sent lawyers and telecommunications regulators scrambling for their English textbooks in a bitter 18-month dispute that serves as an expensive reminder of the importance of punctuation. The construction of a single sentence in the 14-page contract allowed the entire deal to be scrapped. The validity of the contract and the millions of dollars at stake all came down to one point — the second comma in the sentence. "Based on the rules of punctuation," the comma in question "allows for the termination of the [contract] at any time, without cause, upon one-year's written notice," the regulator said. This is a classic case of where the placement of a comma has great importance.

Protect your ass-ets.

If your state has a Bulk Sales Act, make sure you and the seller comply with it before you close your transaction. It's important that creditors of the business receive notice of the owner's intention to sell it. Ask your accountant if the financial records appear to be clean. Get indemnification from the seller.

Here's an example: The city of Chicago enacted a "bulk sale" ordinance. "Before purchasing a business, take the necessary steps to protect yourself from becoming liable for your seller's delinquent taxes and other debts to the city. If you buy a business without notifying the city at least 45 days before the sale, you become responsible for all unpaid city taxes and debts of the seller up to the amount of the purchase price."

Don't steal a seller's business.

Don't steal a seller's business by taking advantage of him when he's down. Your tactic will become known to the competitors of the seller's business. They will not trust you; they fear you are a pirate who will not play fairly, that you may hurt them.

On the other hand, if the seller tells his competitor cronies you paid a fair price, even if it was lower than he might have received had he had more time to find another buyer, these competitors are more likely to play fairly with you AND you might be first to know when a competitor decides to sell.

See your doomsday plan before executing the contract.

Even if you are sure the deal you contemplate will be worthwhile, review your doomsday plan, which you prepared not later than during your business valuation phase. Doing this before an acquisition or merger can help you avoid a troublesome deal. This contingency plan can also show you how you might run away, if necessary, from a disastrous acquisition, minimizing your penalties.

Protect yourself against the seller who skips town.

It is safer for you and better for the business if the previous owner is available to you during your transition into the business. The length of time and the degree of availability and assistance by the seller relates to how long it will take you to be accepted by employees, customers, and suppliers.

Ask but don't expect a test drive.

The owner of a wonderful business won't let a lookiloo into the business. A wise seller will not permit you to observe the business in action until you execute a definitive purchase agreement. Perhaps the final contingency of sale is your reasonable satisfaction with what you see during your day or week on the job. If the seller won't agree to this, it may not be a red flag. Your ability to get an insider's view depends upon the type of business and the rapport between you and the seller.

Being stymied is not necessarily a stalemate.

When you and the seller are still friendly and you both want to do a deal, but you can't make progress because of disagreement, bring in your advisors. Let them speak for you. Perhaps you should ask the seller, too, to step out of the ring and let his advisor talk to your advisor.

Don't reveal your deadline or motivation to buy.

Don't reveal your deadline or motivation to buy to anyone but your *Business Buyer Advocate*. If you tell or give a hint about this to the seller, broker, or anyone else, you probably will regret it. The "other side" will use your urgency, at the last minute, to seek last-minute concessions from you.

Don't go too fast at the end of negotiations.

This tip is not for the faint of heart. It is important you proceed quickly through due diligence and most of dealmaking. If you are sure the seller "loves you" and there are no other buyers on scene (which is impossible if a business broker represents the seller), stall for time the moment you and the seller think you have a deal. By now the seller is exhausted (and so are you). He is visualizing cashing your check and then moving on to whatever is next in his life. Use your advisors to throw a last-minute wrench into the deal.

Delays can kill the deal; keep the ball in motion.

Procrastination is one of the leading causes for deals falling through. The longer it takes to achieve a meeting of the minds between buyers, sellers, their advisors, and sources of financing, the more likely the deal will crater. Dealmaking is like a pendulum. It must stay in motion with activity swinging back and forth between the buyer and seller. Complete stops are not smart.

What is your opportunity cost?

The longer it takes you to buy a business, the higher your opportunity cost. You forego the monthly salary and business profit you could earn from owning a company until you consummate a purchase. You waste money fast.

Example: If it takes you one more week to get started or to meet the next seller of a mature, profitable, fairly priced company, and you would earn $20,000 more per month from your target business, $5,000 is your effective loss (each week!).

A delay in buying can cost you as much as paying too much. It's like standing on the sidelines during a rising real estate or stock market.

Don't be foolish.

Most business owners and their advisors are honest; what you see is what you get. A few, however, will con you if you give them the chance. You can discourage and possibly repel someone who wants to swindle you if you take a few simple precautions.

Don't do business with anyone you don't trust or who has a poor reputation. Don't brandish your greed; it's an opening for exploitation. Demonstrate your legitimacy and tell people you expect it from them. There is a small truth in every big lie, so probe to expand the volume of truth until it overcomes the potential for falsity. Don't take a risk without downside protection. Let people think you are bigger and meaner than you appear, so they don't want to tangle with you.

Are you vulnerable? You might be if you have been swindled or if it is essential for you to buy a business sooner than later.

Using a Business Buyer Advocate.

There is no conflict-of-interest or hidden agenda when you rely upon a professional who is truly an advocate, exclusively, for the buyer. *Business Buyer Advocates* access the hidden market of businesses for sale by-owner (which represents as much as 80% of *profitable* companies that are sold). Lack of business buyer competition and access to the best companies is why prudent buyers want to shop in the hidden market.

Don't fail to detect a wavering seller.

You've heard about buyer remorse. Sellers suffer a similar ailment. Both ailments can pass without harm. As it becomes increasingly clear to the seller that he indeed owns a marketable business that will sell for a good price, he can't help but wonder, "Can I get a better deal from another buyer?" Some owners worry about selling their "baby." Some owners, who have been busy for so long, enjoy the breath of fresh air that you bring to the business and then they decide to keep it. Business buyers naturally focus on the benefits and the potential of the business. This causes some discretionary sellers to postpone the event, which usually means you need to find another business to buy. You can influence this by reminding the seller about how nice it will be for him when he can begin to enjoy what waits for him after he unloads his business on you.

Watch for signs that the owner might withdraw his offer to sell or try to torpedo your buy/sell agreement.

Don't accept a bum's rush.

Don't let the seller burn up the clock at your disadvantage during dealmaking. Your LOI or purchase agreement should specify exactly the information, its format and timing that the seller is supposed to convey to you. If the seller is tardy, your document should provide a means to extend the time clock; otherwise, you can be manipulated into a bad deal or cope with other penalties.

Don't blame the seller.

So, you are in the middle of negotiations and the seller appears to be balking or is dragging his feet on providing data. You don't have enough data to know if the business is right for you. Perhaps the data are sketchy, or the seller's accountant is slow in producing documents. You really want to confront the seller; you are aching to call him out and pin him down and ask him if he really wants to sell. Don't do it.

Don't blame the seller. Instead, blame the loan officer at a mythical bank. Meet with the seller and say: "I've been cooperating with your accountant, but I can't get enough information. I've spoken with several bankers and they all tell me that I don't have enough information to put together a loan application. They want a monthly cash flow by line item. I really want this deal to go through. Can you help me get the data I need to get the loan to pay you what you need?"

Don't give the seller reason to back out of your deal.

Don't inadvertently give a wavering seller an opening to abort the transaction that you contemplate. Properly handle *your* contingencies in the contract, such as deadlines for due diligence, financing, valuation, and legal review.

CHAPTER 8

Closing the Transaction

Escrow and closing the sale / purchase of a company is a critical time in dealmaking. It can be complicated. It is when pending transactions can falter.

This chapter details what is happening and what to do about it.

Understand escrow and closing.

Don't know about escrow and closing? There are six basic stages during the closing/escrow:

- examination and review

- investigation

- document drafting

- signing

- disbursing

- notification and recordation

How do you benefit from escrow? Advantages to utilizing an escrow to close your transaction:

- accuracy

- finality

- neutrality

- cost-effectiveness

- impartiality

Don't close the purchase too soon.

Observe the business for at least one sales cycle; it can range from a week to months. The seller of a good, fairly priced business will not permit delays unless you protect him with provisions in your purchase contract.

Don't ask for early possession.

It is risky for you to take possession of the business before the closing of your purchase transaction. If you break it, you buy it. You can inadvertently harm the business or be accused of damaging it. You can be liable for more by taking control before the closing than you would be if you complete the legal process to close the transaction.

You choose the escrow agent / closing attorney.

No matter how "simple" your acquisition, you need an escrow or settlement company (which may be an attorney) to act as an independent party between you, the seller and organizations that deal with the business (i.e., landlord, lenders, etc.). The correct agent is someone who routinely closes the sale of businesses. The escrow firm that closed the purchase of your home could be your worst choice.

Don't under- or overvalue potential; keep it to yourself.

Keep it to yourself if you see more opportunity for the business than the seller. Your insight might encourage you to make concessions to the seller that would not be reasonable were it not for the strong potential for the business to become more profitable. On the other hand, don't be unrealistically mesmerized by potential.

Don't go it alone.

Consider selling part of the company to capable key employees. It can reduce your risk and substantially increase their productivity.

Who will buy your company when it's time to sell?

You might buy the right business the right way and not be able to sell it. Before you buy, make sure there will be demand for your business from other business buyers within a reasonable period when you try to sell it.

"Buyer Remorse" is normal.

You won't have it before you buy and if you get "buyer remorse" it will be too late to do much about it. Now is a good time to make a list of all the reasons why you want to own your own business. Make another list of your apprehensions. Use your *Business Buyer Advocate* to help you handle your apprehensions. And then go buy a business and rejoice in your new lifestyle. Later, if buyer remorse raises its ugly head, banish it by reviewing your reasons for buying a business and the fact that you bought a good one.

Russell L. Brown, in his book, *Strategies for Successfully Buying or Selling a Business,* says someone will always get cold feet just before the closing! Closing the deal is always difficult but is usually the shortest part of buying or selling an operating business. After all, the valuations, investigations, and negotiations are complete and now it's a matter of getting everything into writing in a form that satisfies everyone so the transfer of ownership of the business can take place. However, you can count on someone getting cold feet just before the closing. Be prepared for this! The seller and buyer may both start to wonder if they are really getting a fair deal. The best way to get ready for this is to anticipate it happening and then to deal logically, reasonably, and unemotionally with it at the time.

Remember who is most influential and when.

Sellers have the most influence and control over buyer behavior before the buyer submits a letter of intent or offer to purchase. Buyers excited about their first impression of the seller and the company can be susceptible to following the seller's or the broker's lead when it comes to the content and timing of the LOI or purchase offer. And that can be a big mistake for the buyer.

Sellers want the buyer to (at least tentatively) commit to a timetable for deal completion, the purchase price and terms, and numerous other things that may not seem important to the buyer. It is not possible for buyers to make informed decisions about the deal until they complete certain parts of due diligence, such as verifying and understanding the firm's methods of accounting and financial reporting.

Unless you, the potential buyer, are certain that legitimate, capable, and motivated buyer competition exists, it is usually not in your self-interest to be too definitive early in your dealmaking. You simply do not know enough about the business. And if there is serious buyer competition, you should ask yourself why you should not move on to another deal where you can be first on scene, which puts you in control so long as you behave fairly and expeditiously process the pending transaction.

As for the LOI, your dealmaking team can make it like glue so the seller wants to give you the first shot at a done deal. You can deploy a LOI, so it works like peeling an onion; make limited commitments subject to seeing limited information about the business, and if you, the buyer, likes what the business discloses, repeat the process, drilling ever more down into the business and making commitments to the seller accordingly. This way the buyer does not fly blindly into a business acquisition, which is how most buyers proceed, and then suffer disappointment when the deal falls through or, worse, when they regret their acquisition.

Don't think a signed contract assures a done deal.

The deal's not done simply because you have a binding agreement.

Most pending deals appear to fall apart several times before closing. This means you must be in the game with your game face on every moment until closing. Expect challenges to your expectations, patience, and tolerance.

Don't forget to ask the most important question.

Before heading off to escrow and signing on the dotted line, did you ask the most important question?

- Is there any information that you have not disclosed to me that might have an adverse bearing on the viability or the value of your business?

You asked the seller this and got verifiable answers to every other question, didn't you?

Did you also ask the seller's representatives and the company's employees, customers, suppliers, landlords, sources of financing?

Business buyers who correctly ask that question at the right time will be gifted (by the respondents) a road map for further inquiry. Not asking that question (and then verifying the response) is why so many dumb deals occur.

If you didn't ask or demand a satisfactory response and document the response in the sale and purchase agreement, it will probably explain your business buying fiasco, which is right around the corner.

CHAPTER 9

When You're in Charge

It is a critical time when you first walk into the company you bought, especially during the first ninety days. You will be overloaded with work. Customers, employees, suppliers and other people and organizations will be anxiously watching you. It's when you discover whether you bought the right business the right way.

This chapter details what is happening and what to do about it.

Do you know what occurs during the transition?

It is essential that you and the seller (and the employees, customers, suppliers, landlord and sources of financing) coordinate to make your transition into the business as smooth as possible. You will get on-the-job experience. It will be like taking a drink from a fire hose. Now that you are the owner (and without causing unnecessary trouble) ask the seller about the itsy-bitsy problems the business has (which he did not mention to you before you bought the business) and which ones you should first address. What should you do about certain employees, customers, or suppliers? Who should be the advisors to the business? What can you immediately do, without adversely affecting the business, to increase revenue and reduce expense? What about inventory? What about customer service? What about marketing? What about finding another business buyer to bail you out? (Just kidding.)

Don't put up with the seller's inadequate assistance.

What if the seller's transitional assistance is inadequate?

Being proactive can empower you to do what the failures can't or won't do to maximize success. Nearly all business buyers are overwhelmed with work and uncertainty during their transition into the company. Nearly all business acquisitions suffer post-acquisition trauma, some of which buyers can avoid, before closing of the purchase transaction, by contracting with the seller for post-acquisition assistance and training, and then after closing enforcing the agreement. Regretfully, too few former owners comply with promises of transitional assistance to the buyer. Sellers that carry paper (finance some of the buyer's purchase) are more likely after closing to provide worthwhile transitional assistance to buyers.

Transitional assistance is especially important if the "value" of goodwill is a significant part of the purchase price. Perhaps as important as the former owner's transitional assistance is the insight and help from the company's employees and the buyer's transition consultant. There are numerous components to manage shortly after closing.

One of the most important is *competitor risk*. You don't want to be blindsided by it. It is usual and customary in some industries for competitors to bad mouth the company or new owner or to make runs at the new owner's key employees and customers. Sometimes a few competitors will gang up on the new owner. And, of course, there is *operational risk*. To what degree must the new owner quickly address internal processes to operate the company at a lower cost or derive more revenue while continuing to provide high-quality customer service and retain good employees?

What about your strategic plan?

Congratulations if you prepared your strategic plan for your company, way back during due diligence and before your done deal. Now is the good time to revisit it and update it based on your now-insider knowledge about your company. If you did not prepare your strategic plan, now is a good time to do it.

Are you being like most business owners, busy handling day-to-day activities and putting out fires?

Don't be like most owners who have not taken the time to look at their business for what it really is—examining the strengths that give it a competitive advantage, and the vulnerabilities that threaten its future. And to do this from the point of view of a potential source of financing or a future business buyer.

Strategic planning helps you unlock the value of your business. The process puts on trial every product, service, and activity of your business.

Start by identifying your business' strengths and weaknesses. And then make decisions on what to do about them and how to exploit your strengths to offset your weaknesses.

The objective is to convert your business from what it is to what it could be.

We use a two-step approach.

First, we conduct a *Business Vitality Checkup*. The purpose is to get an *outsider's* perspective of your business. This will provide us with a three-dimensional (past, present, future) snapshot of your business. The process begins with asking you questions concerning financial, marketing, and strategic analysis. Your answers to these preliminary questions determine the avenues of evaluation, and they provide us with insight as to where your business is going.

The outcome of the checkup is the foundation for a strategic plan.

The second step is creating the Strategic Plan. We design a planning process to suit your business. We help you translate your strategic vision into accelerated action.

The goal is to make your company more profitable and marketable (so someday, when you want to sell, a buyer will pay top dollar).

Six essential elements to a strategic plan.

There are six essential interrelated elements to a strategic plan. Address each simultaneously to minimize surprises and setbacks.

1. **Mission** of your business. What it is and what it wants to become.

2. **Goals** and Objectives. Identify goals for your business and goals for the owners and employees.

3. **Situation** analysis and perception survey. Involve your business' *C.E.L.B.S.* ™ (customers, employees, landlord, bankers, and suppliers).

4. **Strategies** to grow or transform your business.

5. Plans to guide you through the **implementation** of the strategies.

6. **Action** steps to implement the strategic plan.

A *Business Vitality Checkup* widens and lengthens your perspective, so you make better decisions each day.

Keep your eyes and ears on the competition.

There is a lesson in this story:

Once upon a time, a fox and a rabbit were having a "cool one" in the local pub. Talk turned to their common enemy, the hounds of the hunters. The fox rather boastfully stated he held no fear of them because he had so many means of escape. If the hounds should come, he could bolt up into the attic and hide until danger was safely past or quick-as-a-flash he could run out the door and no hound alive could catch him. He could head for the nearest stream and run in it for a spell until the hounds completely lost his scent. He could even go in circles and backtrack a few times and so completely confuse the hounds that he could then climb a tree and watch them in their quandary as they sought to find where he was. Yes, his methods were many and his confidence was high.

On the other hand, the rabbit rather timidly and with some embarrassment confessed that if the hounds should come, he knew only one thing to do, and that was to run like a "scared rabbit."

Well, moments later they heard the baying of the hounds. The rabbit, true to his word, hopped up and ran out the door like a scared rabbit. The fox hesitated --- as he debated whether to bolt up into the attic, dart out the door and depend on his speed, head for the stream, or take off and confuse the hounds by backtracking. While thinking, the hounds rushed in and tore the fox to shreds.

Don't like the mess you're in?

Are your unrealistic expectations coming to roost?

To what degree are you the problem? Try to distinguish the variances between what the seller disclosed to you, the warranties, and representatives, versus what you wish was disclosed and what you discovered when you got control of the business.

Don't panic. Worry (maybe).

Don't swap one paranoia for another. It's normal to worry about your competitors. It's normal to worry about not making enough investment in your marketing and production capacity. It's normal to worry about growing your business, so you can fend off your competitors and make more money. But it is not normal or wise to vacillate between these issues. You can avoid being on the horn of a dilemma if you use this sure-fire way to grow your business and beat the competition. Eat the competition! Buying the competition lets you beat the competition. If you want something worthwhile to worry about, worry about this: You're going backward when you are standing still in business. Don't dally.

Andrew Sloop, managing partner at Nexo Capital Partners, LLC, writes: My first piece of advice for the buyer would be not to panic. This can be an emotional situation for someone who has quite possibly spent their life's savings on purchasing a business that is not what they expected it would be. Often buyer's remorse can quickly spiral into desperation, litigation, finger pointing, and big problems for everyone involved. Whether it be a case of poorly executed due diligence, rash decision making, or false/incomplete information, I feel that the best approach is to dig into finding a solution. Consulting with experienced professionals like those at SCORE would be a good start. Throwing up one's hands in desperation will only make a tough situation worse.

Benefit from the 80/20 Rule.

This topic is adapted from the article, "How the 80/20 Rule Helps Us Be More Effective," by Pinnicle Management Associates.

The "80/20 Rule" is also known as *Pareto's Principle*. It can be an effective tactic to help you effectively manage your resources. The 80/20 Rule means that in anything, a few things (20 percent) are vital, and most things (80 percent) are trivial.

In your warehouse, for example, 20 percent of your stock probably takes up 80 percent of your storage space, and 80 percent of your stock comes from 20 percent of your suppliers. Similarly, 80 percent of your sales will come from 20 percent of your sales staff. 20 percent of your staff will cause 80 percent of your problems, but another 20 percent of your staff will provide 80 percent of your production.

It works both ways. The value of the Pareto Principle for a manager is that it reminds you to focus on the 20 percent that matters. Of the things you do during your day, only 20 percent really matter. Those 20 percent produce 80 percent of your results. Identify and focus on those things.

When the fire drills of the day begin to sap your time, remind yourself of the 20 percent you need to focus on. If something in the schedule must slip, if something isn't going to get done, make sure it's not part of that 20 percent. Helping the good become better is a better use of your time than helping the great become terrific.

Apply the Pareto Principle to all you do but use it wisely.

Don't act before thinking and then collaborating.

Strategic planning is supposed to occur before the acquisition. So should preparation of the business' goals, objectives, operating plan, budgets, etc. Once in control, try to get suggestions and strive to achieve agreement among your employees about what you perceive and about what to do with your company's strengths, weaknesses, opportunities, and threats (SWOT).

Changing anything too soon is risky.

Assuming you bought a mature, profitable business, do not be too quick to change anything without a good reason. Whatever the business has been doing is working; that is why it has competitive advantages, has profit, and has potential. It's why you bought the business.

Don't "fix" what works.

Too many people incorrectly assume a business can do better if it changes its strategy and tactics.

Look first at how well people implement strategies and tactics. The problem usually relates to how people perform their jobs. To discover this, it is necessary to interview customers, employees, sources of financing, suppliers and outside professionals who have advised the company. It is not reliable to interview the person in question because all of us operate behind rose-colored glasses.

Don't make too many simultaneous changes.

Too many buyers, once in control of their company, overwhelm their business or offend its relationships when they shake up how things are done. It's a good way to lose the best employees and to trouble or repel customers and suppliers. It's better to carefully evaluate, while conferring with stakeholders, and then plan and communicate your rationale for changes. Stay in contact with the affected people to observe their reactions and, accordingly, modify your plans. Be particularly careful about deploying disruptive innovations; they tend to disrupt longer than people anticipate. The last part of implementation can be more aggravating and take longer than all the work preceding it. It's usually better to establish your creds and nourish relationships before you expect people to jump onto your band wagon. Collaborate more than pronounce. We have a saying: "Go slow to go fast."

Don't be needlessly risk averse.

A funny thing happens to some buyers who courageously venture into the business acquisition arena; they turtle when they own a company. Fear of failure causes too many failures. Taking too long to make decisions or not aggressively striving for bigger and better is a formula for mediocrity.

Don't delay striking back at the seller.

The seller didn't produce adequate records, right?

You asked for the information (didn't you?) but you didn't get it, or it was not sufficient. Besides not having enough worthwhile information to make an informed decision about purchasing the company, if it turns out your business buying attempt is a disaster, you might not have sufficient documentation to use against the seller and other parties to the transaction.

Don't jump from the frying pan into the fire.

Buyer wants out—now! But wait . . . Here's insight from a dealmaker:

"If a deal isn't misrepresented and the buyer did competent due diligence, you have to wonder what they were thinking. Let's assume that the person found out they were very sick and just wanted out. Seven options:

1. obtain the names of potential buyers that were interested in buying the business; offer it to them

2. list the business for sale

3. negotiate with an employee to manage the business

4. hire a professional manager

5. sell to the employees through an ESOP

6. fire sale and take a loss

7. shut the business or give it away"

Dennis Zink, Change Agent, Business Alchemist

Look for alternatives for getting out of a deal.

Maybe you can sell the business.

Here's an example provided by a dealmaker:

"Had this happen. A professional real estate property manager in another state bought a residential property management business, which was one of my listings. When the buyer relocated to Texas, her first impressions of the business, and other things, were not up to snuff. She came to me for advice. Tip: Have a disgruntled buyer go back to the broker who did the deal and see if an arrangement can be made to connect the actual buyer to the listing broker's connections to other potential buyers that were interested in the same business. In my case, there was another buyer who'd made a counteroffer; I told the disgruntled buyer about it. She contacted the person who earlier wanted to buy the business. She sold the business to him. I was paid on the original buy/sell transaction, but I did not ask for another fee because I was glad to help. I gained the goodwill from the "assist." Business buyers who want to try this might have to pay a "referral fee" to the original broker to cooperate in such a transaction."

David J. Sweeten, CBI, CPA, BCB, LREB, Business Brokers of Texas, Inc.

Don't dither making important decisions.

Everyone in and outside the company is monitoring the new owner. Involve the key employees as you begin to make corrections and improvements so everyone realizes that you run a team; dispensing edicts from your office can turn already nervous employees into fearsome and self-protective employees.

Don't confuse spending with investing.

A dollar spent is a dollar lost unless it produces more than a dollar of revenue. Do not spend money unless you know how the expenditure will increase sales or reduce costs. It is naive to believe you are getting a valuable tax write-off when you spend money. Spend a dollar, and at most you save fifty cents in taxes, but in fact you are still fifty cents poorer than had you not spent the money. Control your overhead. It is easy to incur expenses that seem reasonable in themselves, yet cumulatively add up to more than you can afford.

Screen accounts payable.

When a business changes hands an opening exists for unscrupulous vendors to pad invoices and for you to receive statements from vendors from which your business does not purchase. Verify the legitimacy of every account payable.

Strengthen computer protection.

Assume that nobody has paid enough attention to computer efficiency and security. Review the programs and files. Use software utilities to test for defects and inefficiencies. Install (or update) shields against viruses and unauthorized access. Spyware, adware, and malware programs are a virulent plague on the Internet; they invade your computer, so they can track and report your activity without your knowledge. Special software exists to counter these evil doers. Restrict the seller's access to computers *immediately* upon closing your purchase transaction. Change passwords; eliminate backdoors, etc.

"Researcher Discovers Superfish Spyware Installed on Lenovo PCs," by Nicole Perlroth, February 2015, *New York Times*: Lenovo, the Chinese tech giant, was shipping PCs with spyware that tracks its customers' every move online, and it renders the computers vulnerable to hackers. Lenovo, the world's largest PC manufacturer, was installing Superfish, a particularly pernicious form of adware that siphons data from a user's machine via web browser. Banking and e-commerce sites, or any web page that purports to be secure with the image of a tiny padlock, are made vulnerable. Citing bad user reviews, the company said it stopped including the adware. "The problem is: what can we trust?"

Create and improve websites.

Until you can afford to spend more, good websites can be created for a few thousand dollars. The monthly hosting fee for a simple site is below $25. Internet analysts say that 25% of all shopping-related searches are for local products and services. Invest a day or two so your website can state your presence, announce sales and special events, describe the features and benefits that your customers enjoy, post testimonials, offer free useful advice, answer frequently asked questions, and provide various means of contact.

Don't be a one-man/woman show.

Your proven strengths should be the basis for the job description that you reserve for yourself. Delegate to other people tasks you are too busy to handle, don't want to handle or can't perform as well as someone else.

Try to work yourself out of the job.

You bought a job, did you? Start thinking about how you can get out of the grind to focus more on planning and supervision.

It is not a good enough reason to buy a business because people hate their job or cannot find another one. Buying a job is a way to jump from the frying pan into the fire. A worthwhile business acquisition should fairly compensate (at market rates) the working owner for managing the company, and provide a decent return on invested capital, and return the capital investment to the purchaser. Anything less is questionable, to say the least. Keep in mind that the smallest businesses are the riskiest to own.

Don't under-utilize employees during transition.

Don't underestimate the value of key employees for your smooth transition. Verify the seller's assurances that the employees are happy, and they will stay after you buy the business. If you or the seller slights employees during the buy/sell or transition process, you could cause morale problems that may harm your business.

Don't be too dependent.

It is risky to be too dependent on key employee(s).

Like customer / revenue concentration, key employee concentration poses business risks. Cross-training of employees is one way to keep the business running smoothly if a key employee quits. Another is to (reasonably) do what it takes so the key employee wants to perform at peak capacity. Establish a succession plan so someone else can step in for absent or departed employees.

It is risky to be too dependent on key supplier(s). Suppliers demanding better terms are not uncommon when a company changes hands. Supplier-competition is the antidote to unreasonable demands from vendors.

Don't minimize the importance of face.

When the "face" of the company about-faces, what then?

It's not always the company owner that the marketplace perceives to be the "face" of the company. It might be someone in marketing or technology or customer service. Companies flying high can quickly go into a tailspin if a material change of behavior arises that causes the company's previously marvelous spokesperson (the face) to pivot in the wrong direction, which adversely affects company's perceived capability and marketplace reputation.

During early 2015 NBC News experienced such an event when *Brian Williams* its principal news figurehead, the anchorman for the dominant *Nightly News with Brian Williams*, according to the *New York Times*, "Embattled Anchor Faces 'Fact-Checking' Inquiry at NBC," admitted on-air that he misled the public with a harrowing tale of a helicopter landing in Iraq. "In addition to tarnishing Mr. Williams's once pristine reputation, the scandal has led to broader questions about the management and the credibility of NBC's news operations." Exasperating the public criticism of NBC was its chief medical editor, Dr. Nancy Snyderman, who violated a self-imposed quarantine after being exposed to Ebola in Liberia, which was on the heels of NBC's removing David Gregory as the host of *Meet the Press*. The *Times* goes on to speculate, "Should Mr. Williams be forced to step down, it is not clear who a successor would be."

It's not good for business when the "face" of the company about-faces or falls on his face. And it's not good if the company has not worked on its succession plans, for the owner, key employees, and key stakeholders.

Don't let electronics undermine your company.

This topic is adapted from an e-newsletter sent by John Martinka, *Business Buyer Advocate*:

I've lately seen a plethora of articles on the numerous devices people use all the time to connect to technology. Wear this, embed that, bury your face in your phone, etc.

So, what's the problem? Business owners and corporate managers are telling me that one of their complications with employees is getting them to make personal contact with customers, including salespeople who prefer to text or email customers and prospects instead of picking up the phone and calling them (or going out to see them).

I like technology. But electronic communication, too often, is the easy way out. "Oh, I emailed them" is the lazy salesperson's way.

I see the same thing with prospective clients and with people who want to network with me. They email me and ask about "next steps." Well, I can write a lengthy response, miss the mark, and waste a lot of time. Or we can talk so I can correctly answer their questions.

It's easy for customers to ignore email. True, they can ignore voicemail but they are more likely to return the call (than respond to email) so you can add the personal touch.

I don't care how much technology we have, the personal touch, by phone and especially in-person, provides so much more value and gets much better results.

By insisting on communicating by email, corporations often reproduce the sort of evasive behavior that incenses customers.

— David Segal, "The Haggler"

Don't forget who is boss.

Is your # 2 employee a problem?

The book you're reading has reminded you about the importance and value of a dedicated, competent, and enthusiastic second-in-command. But sometimes that employee's enthusiasm gets out of hand when the company changes hands. It's a good idea to reward enthusiasm but it is not a good idea to let your #2 employee exert too much control over you or the company. This arises, sometimes, because that employee overcompensates for what s/he perceives to be your nervousness during your transition into the company or your business management shortcomings.

Longstanding rivalries between your #2 and one or more other employees can escalate now that the former owner is gone; you probably don't know enough about the company's politics. Be cautious taking sides.

Romance the best; dump the rest.

Employees, customers, and suppliers are the most important business actors. Do things that favorably impress them immediately after your acquisition. And particularly nourish the highest performing employees and suppliers. While you are relationship-building with your key employees, ask them to what extent they think you should weed out the worst employees. Chances are they will encourage this because slackers and incompetents usually make more work for the best employees.

"Change employees or change employees" is a slogan from turnaround expert, Lou Sammartano, Full Circle Worldwide Consulting, LLC.

One of the best resources on this topic is the book, *Great Employees Only*, by Dale Dauten.

Don't take it out on your employees.

Especially when you are transitioning into your business acquisition, when you are in a bad mood, don't take it out on your staff. Take it out on your family. Just kidding! Your financial security can be at stake if you abuse your employees. Don't let your personal problems become your workers' problems.

Hire employees who need the job.

The best employees I hired were desperate for the kind of job I offered, and they were more productive and loyal to my company than were employees being sought by my competitors. Part-time employees will strive for a full-time position, which is another reason part-timers should be in your employee mix.

Making yourself crazy can make others crazy, too.

If money can fix it, it's not a problem worth worrying about. Don't be depressed about a flat tire; pay someone to fix it so you can be on your way. An incurable malignant tumor? That's a different story—all the money in the world can't fix that.

Form strategic alliances to strengthen advantages.

An *INC. Magazine* article, "The Declaration of Independents," says forming alliances is an increasingly important way to accelerate growth, access new competencies, and enter new markets, according to Marc S. Margulis, managing director of the corporate alliances group at the investment banking services firm of Houlihan Lokey Howard & Zukin in Los Angeles. "The question is no longer, 'Should I consider an alliance?' Now the questions are much more interesting than that. They include, 'What form should the alliance take?' and 'How do I find the right partner?'" Choose your partner carefully because CEOs surveyed about failed alliances said their biggest mistake was choosing the first partner who came along. "Dating is the best way to find out who's the best partner," Margulis said.

Example: Many states strive for an "open roads" policy, which means they encourage law enforcement and tow truck operators to expedite the clearing of an accident scene, so motorists are impeded as little as possible. So, they could be included in the selection process when one state selected towing operators, several small companies cooperated to form a new business enterprise. Its specialty is to contract with the state with respect to its quick-clearance program. These small competitors formed a strategic business alliance because none of them could afford the capital investment in additional equipment that the state required to be a state approved contractor. These firms did not give up their respective businesses; they continue to compete as usual. Their alliance simply enables them to access a bigger customer and share in the profit from this customer.

Don't wait to warn customers.

Fess up so you don't have to kiss up. Provide your customers with a heads up and apology when you know they are not going to be pleased with something you have done or are delivering to them.

Keep your eye on the landlord and property manager.

There are so many ways landlords cause problems for tenants. We've seen dozens of them, but there isn't enough space in this book to showcase all of them. So, here are a few things to think about:

- Landlords might approve the lease assignment but might not cooperate on renewals. Nail this down before buying.

- Did the landlord comply with the lease before you bought the business? If not, don't expect improvement.

- Does the lease permit the landlord to lease to your competitors?

- Don't allow the landlord an unrestricted right to relocate you within the building or building complex at the convenience of the landlord.

- Document how much money and when the landlord compensates you for a move dictated by the landlord.

- Don't agree to pay the landlord disputed amounts before they are resolved.

- You may be at risk if your landlord loses the building in foreclosure. Does your lease protect the tenant (you)?

- The tenant should have recourse when the building is not maintained according to written expectations.

Don't let the seller drop the ball.

A business is "sold" in the owner's mind before he sells it to you. His short-timer attitude can adversely affect the business. Watch for signs that the seller is slacking off, especially as it pertains to maintaining the goodwill of the business. Encourage the seller to make one last effort, before he leaves, to strengthen the business' relationship with its employees, customers, suppliers, landlord(s), and sources of financing. Similarly, discourage the seller from committing the company to material promises, obligations or changes to policies and procedures that significantly change the way the firm does business. It's wise for the buyer and seller to agree that neither one will issue a news release to announce the sale without the prior approval of the other (which won't be unreasonably withheld). Appeal to the seller's desire to do the right thing, which includes your self-interest. This may avert problems and it *will* smooth your way into the business.

Don't be too quick to jump ship.

Don't let your lack of persistence be the reason for failure. It takes longer for some types of businesses to solve problems or increase profit. Don't give up until you are certain you have tried everything to make it work. Of course, a business plan helps because it enables you to test decisions without the risk you assume when you test a decision in actual operations.

Are you between the devil and the deep blue sea?

This topic comes from Ron Sturgeon's book, *Jargon and All the Stuff You Really Can't Do Without,* referring to "a decision-making situation when all alternatives are unpleasant or undesirable. This is like being between a rock and a hard place. Indeed, would you rather have a meeting with the devil or the deep blue sea?" His example of someone in such a predicament:

"We were faced with continuing the old product line that was still breaking even or dumping it and starting over with a more expensive but more promising lineup of new products. We were caught between the devil and the deep blue sea."

Don't wait to shut down.

Going out of business is not as bad as it can get. It is worse to take a long time to fail, all the while losing money. It's natural to try to save face by holding onto your poor investment. But it is wiser to cut your loss and sell or shut down your loser.

Each month accurately assess whether your business is worth more than it was last month. If it is not or if you are in doubt, do a shut-down analysis. Do not throw good money after bad. Optimism is fine, but don't jeopardize your personal financial security by unwisely transferring your savings into your company.

Keep dreaming.

Your first business acquisition does not have to be your last. Once you are comfortable with your company, begin to look for your next acquisition. You might merge your business with another one; you might acquire another business. You might sell your company so that you can trade up for a bigger, more profitable one.

Don't worry, be happy!

You deserve it. Congratulations on your desire to realize your dream of business ownership. Good luck and be safe!

You did it! Congratulations.

And best wishes for your continued success!

Thank you for using this book to buy the *right* business the *right* way.

To be continued . . . I'm not done writing about this topic.

CHAPTER 10

How to Prepare and Find the Right Business to Buy

You've been reading: *How to **Buy** the Right Business the Right Way.*

Knowing *how* to buy is important. But, if you haven't *found* at least one (more is better) of the best businesses for sale, you may end up buying the *wrong* business the *right* way.

If you're not sure you know everything you need to know so you can adequately prepare and present yourself and then efficiently identify the best-of-the-best potential acquisitions, read my other book:

- *How to **Prepare** Yourself and **Find** the **Right** Business to **Buy**.*
- The next few pages highlight some of the topics in that book.

Get started right.

One of the most crucial things in searching for a company to buy is to get started right. You only have one chance to make a favorable first impression. If you don't have all the components in place before you meet the owner of a good business, you could blow your chance to buy it.

- First impression. The best companies for sale are typically mishandled by the buyer during the first seller contact. There are two sales being made from the first moment. The seller is trying to sell you his business and you are trying to sell yourself (remember, you're effectively applying for the job of company president).

Few people setting out to buy a company know the best ways to showcase what they bring to the table, such as their resume, financial capability, advisory team, acquisition criteria. Without expert knowledge about searching for worthwhile companies for sale (or that could be for sale if properly approached), it's not possible to access all the opportunities, especially the best businesses for sale on the hidden market.

Know what you are up against.

The first step is to know what you are up against. And then you can mitigate the risks and exploit the opportunities. You can make your and everyone else's jobs easier while you are interacting with people and organizations on your way to buying the right business the right way. You can encourage an environment of collaboration instead of confrontation.

Preparing and searching to buy a business.

This topic is covered in my other book: *How to Prepare Yourself and Find the Right Business to Buy.*

It will help you understand the processes and challenges as you plan your purchase of a company.

The first step to buying a company is finding one you want to buy. You'll learn how to do it, so you can avoid pitfalls along the way.

Searching in the public market is like rowing a boat with one oar; it takes a lot of effort and you don't get far.

Learn how to access the unadvertised and huge hidden market of sellers, which is where to find the best companies and the best deals.

Why settle for some of the businesses for sale if you can access all of them?

Afterword

Here's how this book came into being and how it evolved over the decades.

Let's start with my admission. I was snookered when I bought the *right* business the *wrong* way—proving the saying: Success does not always breed success.

I've guided hundreds of buyers as they acquired mature, profitable, fairly priced companies having sustainable competitive advantages. I've purchased or invested in twenty-nine small or midsize businesses. Twenty-eight were winners. But early in my career I took a bath on one of them. So, how I did I get snookered? My dream became a nightmare because, before I bought it, I did not do a good enough job investigating the seller and the company.

Had I adequately deployed the due diligence process, which I use with my clients (some of it summarized in this book), I might have detected the risks before I closed on my misguided transaction. My legal team got me out of the mess thanks to my well-drafted purchase and sale agreement. I lost money, sure, but it could have been much worse.

I pledged, from then on, to devote most of my business life to helping people avoid mistakes so they could profit from business ownership. Since my disastrous acquisition, I've been noting mistakes people make during their business buying activity, some of which I observed while consulting with clients; other errors were reported to me by the independent professional advisors trained in the use of my trade secrets, know-how and dealmaking tools.

What you read in this book comprises less than 10% of what is in the materials available to our *Business Buyer Advocates*˚. Their materials and client reference guides show how to handle various tasks, using our proprietary methodologies and our data gathering and analysis forms.

Contact me for help at PartnerOnCall.com.

Acknowledgements

How to Buy the Right Business the Right Way
How to Prepare Yourself and Find the Right Business to Buy

The *Dos, Don'ts & Profit Strategies*, in those books, and my success, would not be as large if not for these people. I don't know everything about buying the *right* business the *right* way, but I know enough dealmakers with state-of-the art expertise to whom I can turn when I need facts, tips, and strategies.

Thank you, first, to my tolerant and supportive wife, **Kathy**, who has put up with me since the 1970s, during my three retirements, and with me becoming bored and going back to work despite her telling me to play more and work less.

John Martinka, MBA, known as "The Escape Artist," since 1993 has been a valuable contributor to my success. He helped establish "Partner" On-Call Network, LLC, taking time away (five years!) from his successful consulting practice to train and collaborate with people we trained to use our system of consulting. His e-newsletter, *Getting the Deal Done,* is in my inbox. His two books are on my desktop: *Buying a Business That Makes You Rich* and *If They Can Sell Pet Rocks Why Can't You Sell Your Business (For What You Want)?*

Robert Nice, a highly successful financial analyst, company manager, real estate investor and consultant, all before beginning to use our system of consulting in 1995, inspires me whenever he empowers people to buy the right business the right way, or helps clients improve and then later profitably exit their companies.

A few more, in alphabetic order:

- **Alan Fox**, who used our dealmaking tools and know-how to acquire a mid-market size company, the revenue of which he quadrupled. And then sold for a BIG profit. He became a *Business Buyer Advocate* in 1998. For several years he outper-formed all of us with respect to income and diversity of trans-actions. He has helped clients buy, start, improve, finance, value and sell small and midsize businesses.

- **Steven Beal**, MBA, CGA, CFA, CBV, CBI, in 2005 was the first Canadian we trained to use our consulting materials. He went on to diversify his business buyer advisory and business improvement consulting practice to include business broker-age. His example encouraged me to train business brokers and other professionals.

- **Bob Biggerstaff**, "Serial Entrepreneur," founded and man-aged several companies one of which was recognized by *INC. Magazine 500* and earned the *Ernst and Young Entrepreneur of the Year Award*. In 2008, after briefly trying but becoming bored with retirement, we trained him. By 2013 his consult-ing firm had grown and diversified beyond the scope of work most of us perform. While not presently a member of our network his influence on us continues to benefit us.

- **David Barnett**, a Canadian we trained to use of our consult-ing materials, helped "Canadianize" for Canadian readers my creative financing book, *How to Get ALL the Money You Want For Your Business Without Stealing It*™, which until the "trans-lation" did not include topics that are Canadian-specific.

- **David Sweeten**, CBI, CPA, BCB, LREB, owner of a business brokerage, was the first brokerage we authorized to use our business consulting materials. Ideas he shares enable me to relate better to the "other side" of the dealmaking table, business brokers, from my buyer-side view of transactions.

- **Fayaz Karim**, BSc, MBA, CPA, Chartered Accountant (Canada), residing / working in the USA, since 2002 has provided me with useful and truthful insight into what really happens within franchise systems. He uses our consulting materials to diversify his longstanding franchise development and consulting activities to include *Business Buyer Advocacy*.

- **Howard Katz** took our training in 1995. It didn't take long for him to do two things that materially increased his success and my success. Within a few months using our consulting methodologies he expanded and monetized one of our client services, which before then I viewed as a minor byproduct of our consulting. His success motivated our *Business Buyer Advocates* to emulate his methods, which substantially increased their income and better-served their clients. He was the first among us to use our consulting know-how to purchase a company for his own account. From that point onward, I have encouraged people in our business to consult AND buy and sell companies for their own account.

- **John Gallagher**, CPA, owned a thriving accounting and tax practice. In 1995 he decided to diversify deeper into business buyer advisory, using our proprietary tools. And then he showed us the power of our know-how when he, over several years, between consulting engagements, bought and sold numerous companies for his own account.

- **Loren Marc Schmerler**, a Certified Professional Consultant and Accredited Professional Consultant, helps business owners understand and maximize their bottom line. His newsletter has given me ideas I have put to successful use.

About the Author

Business Buyer Advocacy ™ and the *Hidden* Marketplace

The goal of *"Partner" On-Call Network* ˚ (and the people we train to become advisors to business buyers) is to facilitate the safe, profitable transfer of businesses, as quickly as possible—so every party to the transaction gets a win-win deal.

In the 1970s, Ted Leverette figured out how to access the "hidden" market of the best small and midsize businesses quietly for sale by-owner. This is important because most business buyers access only about 20% of the mature and profitable companies for sale, the ones represented by brokers or advertised to the public. When those buyers find sellers on the "public" market, they are among a horde of buyers who congregate around those sellers. These buyers can cause a bidding war among themselves, which means businesses can sell for more than they are worth (which is a good thing if you want to *sell* your business).

Of course, Leverette had to have a name for his discovery of the way to introduce buyers to the best businesses for sale, of which up to 80% are on the *hidden* market. And then guide buyers through evaluation and dealmaking, with loyalty only to the buyer. So, he coined and trademarked an advisory title: *Business Buyer Advocate* ˚.

The idea worked well for many years, so Leverette decided to teach other people how to consult with business buyers. These consultants use his trade secrets, know-how and dealmaking tools in their independently owned and operated consulting practices in the USA and Canada.

Their 500-year collective experience gives their clients more leverage than is otherwise possible.

"Partner" On-Call Network LLC is not a business brokerage; we don't list businesses for sale and then take them to market; independent users of our information might be. We collaborate with and recommend the best brokers. Brokers reciprocate by referring clients.

Also by Ted Leverette

How to Prepare Yourself and Find the Right Business to Buy ™

How to Get ALL the Money You Want For Your Business Without Stealing It ™

21st Century Entrepreneur Ideas for Kids and Aspirational Adults ™

120 Financial Lifelines for Small Businesses ™

Food & Fun on the Central Coast™

The Best of the Central Coast™

Some of these books are available only to the clients and users of the "Partner" On-Call Network LLC proprietary system of consulting:

- The Street-Smart Way to Become a Business Consultant™
- Business Buyer Training Syllabus™
- Business-For-Sale Locating & Screening System™
- Business Acquisition System™
- Business Profit Maximizer™
- Business Seller Training Syllabus™
- Preparing a Business for Sale™
- The Street-Smart System to Start a Business™
- *Franchise Evaluation and Selection System*™

List of Topics